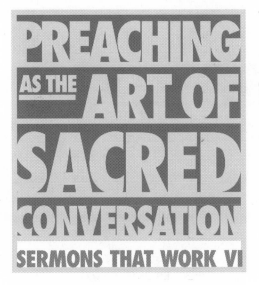

PREACHING AS THE ART OF SACRED CONVERSATION

SERMONS THAT WORK VI

edited by
Roger Alling and David J. Schlafer

MOREHOUSE PUBLISHING
HARRISBURG, PENNSYLVANIA

Morehouse Publishing

Editorial Office:
871 Ethan Allen Hwy.
Ridgefield, CT 06877

Corporate Office:
P.O. Box 1321
Harrisburg, PA 17105

ISBN 0-8192-1699-2

A catalog record for this book is available from the
Library of Congress.

Printed in the United States of America

CONTENTS

SECTION III

SECTION IV

CONTRIBUTORS

Ten of the sermons presented in this book were winners in the 1996 Best Sermon Competition sponsored by The Episcopal Evangelism Foundation. Those winners in order are as follows:

The Rev. Jonathan E. Currier, St. Christopher's Church, New Carrollton, MD
The Rev. Dayle Casey, Chapel of Our Savior, Colorado Springs, CO
The Rev. James W. Law, All Souls Episcopal Church, Oklahoma City, OK
The Rev. James Adams, Episcopal High School, Alexandria, VA
The Rev. Rick Oberheide, McChord AFB Chapel, McChord AFB, WA
The Rev. William J. Eakins, Trinity Episcopal Church, Hartford, CT
The Rev. Beth Wickenberg Ely, All Saints Episcopal Church, Charlotte, NC
The Rev. Margaret Schwarzer, Trinity Church, Princeton, NJ
The Rev. Meredith Woods Potter, One in Christ Episcopal Church,
      Park Ridge, IL
The Rev. Nathaniel Pierce, Christ Episcopal Church, Cambridge, MD

The other preachers represented in the book, all staff members at the 1996 Preaching Excellence Program, are the following:

The Rev. Roger Alling
The Episcopal Evangelism Foundation, Inc.

The Rev. Anne K. Bartlett
Parish of St. John the Baptist, Portland, Oregon

The Most Rev. Edmond L. Browning
Presiding Bishop, The Episcopal Church

The Rev. Linda Clader
The Church Divinity School of the Pacific

The Rev. Mitties McDonald De Champlain
The Fuller Theological Seminary

The Rev. William Hethcock
The School of Theology, Sewanee, Tennessee

The Rev. Debra Metzgar
Holy Innocents Episcopal Church, Atlanta, Georgia

The Rev. Joy E. Rogers
St. Thomas Episcopal Church, Battle Creek, Michigan

The Rev. Eugene Sutton
The Diocese of New Jersey

The Rev. Tom Troeger
The Iliff School of Theology, Denver, Colorado

The Rev. J. Donald Waring
St. Thomas Episcopal Church, Terrace Park, Ohio

EDITORS

Roger Alling is president of the Episcopal Evangelism Foundation, which oversees both the annual Preaching Excellence Program for Episcopal Seminarians, and the nationwide call for sermons that are eventually published in this volume. A parish priest for many years, he has also served as stewardship officer for the Diocese of Connecticut. He is the editor of *Sermons That Work V: Distinctive Dimensions of Anglican Preaching* (Forward Movement, 1995).

David J. Schlafer is adjunct professor of homiletics at Virginia Theological Seminary. He leads conferences for preachers in a wide variety of institutional settings, as well as working with individuals and small colleague groups on their preaching. He has previously served as a professor of preaching at Nashotah House, Seabury-Western, the University of the South, and has been Interim Director of Studies at the College of Preachers. He is the author of *Surviving the Sermon: A Guide to Preaching for Those Who Have to Listen*, and *Your Way with God's Word: Discovering Your Distinctive Preaching Voice*, both published by Cowley Publications. Another book, *What Makes This Day Different? Preaching Grace on Special Occasions*, will be published by Cowley early in 1997. Along with Roger Alling, he is editor of *Sermons That Work V*.

FOREWORD

In recent years, many people have come to realize that a viable civilization must be based on morality, and morality has no solid foundation but religion. Still, none of us is born with a complete understanding of God. Christians need considerable and continual help to understand and put into practice the breadth of their faith.

This help can come from many sources, and one of them is preaching—excellent preaching, that is. Poor sermons can not only hinder Christians but can drive them out of the church and into the ranks of the church's alumni.

The mission of the Episcopal Evangelism Foundation is to improve preaching in the Episcopal Church, and this book contains the fruits of some of our efforts. This year, as in the past five, we invited the clergy in all of the church's parishes to submit their best sermons. The entries were judged by the Foundation's board of directors, and the top five winners, as well as their parishes, received cash prizes that were made possible by the generosity of John C. Whitehead, former deputy secretary of state and an active Episcopalian. As in the past, this book contains those winning sermons, as well as the five runners up.

I hope you enjoy reading these prize-winning sermons as well as the sermons and addresses delivered by the faculty and guests at our ninth annual Preaching Excellence Program, held in June in Columbus, Ohio. Each year nearly fifty seminarians who show outstanding promise in preaching are selected by the deans and homiletics professors of all eleven Episcopal seminaries. They spend an intensive week on the art and practice of preaching, led by five homiletics professors and five skilled parish preachers, in addition to well-known guest lecturers including, this year, the Reverend Thomas Troeger, professor of homiletics at the Iliff School of Theology in Denver and a noted preacher and author, and the Reverend Dr. Walter Bouman, professor of theology at Trinity Lutheran Seminary and a leading participant in the current Episcopal-Lutheran dialogue. We were especially happy that the Most Reverend Edmond L. Browning, Presiding Bishop of the Episcopal Church, and the Reverend Dr. Daniel P. Matthews, rector of Trinity Church, Wall Street, both made special trips to Columbus to address the Conference.

I believe that the sermons in this book show that preaching in the Episcopal Church has gotten much better, but there is still room for more improvement. Please help us to raise further the level of preaching in the church with your suggestions and tax-deductible contributions.

A. Gary Shilling
Chairman
The Episcopal Evangelism Foundation, Inc.
500 Morris Avenue
Springfield, NJ 07081
(201) 467-0070

PREFACE

"God's Spirit Bears Witness with Our Spirits"
The Conversation Partners of Inspired Preaching

One thing about preaching seems to be perfectly clear—all you have to do is to watch and listen to it a couple of times: preaching is a religious monologue. There stands the preacher, alone in the pulpit (or the aisle), a solitary proponent of religious truth claims—about God and the word, judgment and mercy, sin and salvation, sacred doctrine and moral practice. Sermons may be long or short, simple or complex, more or less interesting or orthodox. They may or may not be taken seriously by those to whom they are addressed. Regardless, however, it is almost always one person up in front, doing the talking.

The "dialogue sermon" was a trendy homiletical trick some preachers tried a few years ago. But the phenomenon had a short life. Dialogue sermons don't crop up very often these days in the Sunday worship patterns of most churches. Preaching appears, quite clearly, to be a solo performance. (And, judging by the glazed eyes and shuffling feet of certain congregations, preaching sometimes even seems to be a soliloquy!)

But appearances can be deceiving. Much more may be going on than seems to be the case on the surface. *Good preaching*, in fact, is *never* merely a monologue. It is, instead, an artfully orchestrated *sacred conversation*.

That observation requires a bit of explaining, for it conflicts with more than casual first impressions. Serious theological eyebrows can be raised in response to it as well.

"We do not proclaim ourselves," St. Paul says most emphatically to the Christians in Corinth. "We proclaim Jesus Christ as Lord, and ourselves as your slaves for Jesus' sake." *That* doesn't sound very much like a "conversation!"

A sermon may not exactly be a "monologue" in the conventional sense of that term. But neither is it the religious equivalent of a TV talk show, a "bull session," a cozy chitchat, a debate, or the reported consensus of a committee meeting.

Faithful preachers, some would insist, have a Ghost Writer. It is the voice of God's Holy Spirit that needs to be heard through the words of the sermon. Sermons should not be moral or theological axe-grinding by the preacher. They should not be psychological itch-scratching for the congregation. Preaching should not be opinion sharing among those who like to talk about religion. No—the sermon should bear witness, neither to the wisdom, eloquence, or sanctity of the human speaker, nor to samplings of sentiment currently making the rounds on the religious talk circuit. Rather, the sermon should bear witness to the Word of God. The long prophetic tradition in which preachers stand has always said—for better or worse—in fear and trembling: "Thus saith the *Lord!*"

"The preacher as herald" is probably too antiquated an image for contemporary consciousness. Perhaps, however, it would not be too farfetched to suggest that the task of the preacher is to serve as a well-calibrated fax machine. The Word of the Lord has come down to us through the words of prophets and apostles, and is recorded in the words of Sacred Scripture. It is the preacher's business to transmit that Word directly and to do so with as few smudges, stray marks, and distracting lines as possible.

Such an image does provide a clear and vivid means for envisioning the nature of God's revelation and for understanding the practice of preaching. *And yet*, this clarity is achieved at the high cost of a seriously restricted theological vision. The prophet or the preacher who faithfully bears witness to the Word of the Lord is *not* just a fax machine. God's commands, at various times and places, may be straightforward and uncompromising. God's Word, however, has *never* been a flat and simple matter of "Now hear this!"

Over and over again in the sacred stories of our faith tradition, God is described as talking *with*, as listening *to*, as deeply honoring the personalities of the human partners with whom God engages in dialogue. According to certain Scripture texts, God even changes his divine (and supposedly immutable) mind as a result of some of these conversational encounters.

Abraham bargains with God—successfully—on behalf of his troublesome nephew Lot. Moses convinces God to give up on a plan to eradicate all the rebellious children of Israel and begin the Grand Covenant Project all over again with Moses alone. The humble sack-cloth-and-ashes repentance of the Ninevites alters God's declared intention of imminent doom (a change-of-plans scenario that Jonah both anticipates and does not appreciate at all). "Come now, and let us reason together," God often says—even when the respondents are ornery and utterly *un*reasonable. "I have heard the cry of my people in Egypt," God declares at the outset of his interchange with Moses at the burning bush.

This divine respect for the distinctively human voice is further manifested in the bold marks of individual authorial personality that are indelibly imprinted throughout the pages of Scripture. The same Paul who declares that he is proclaiming "not himself, but Christ," for instance, quite often goes on at great length about his own ideas and experiences—transparently displaying his peripatetic mind and his volatile temperament in the process.

How do we know that we are children of God? Not, according to St. Paul, because God says, "Shut up and listen! Don't talk back!" but rather because God's Spirit *bears witness with our spirits* that we are children of God.

Illustrations of this pattern—invited human influence in the process of divine revelation—can easily be multiplied. The prophet Amos is a dirt-poor tree surgeon. And he embodies a no-nonsense cutting edge in his incisive analysis and trenchant critique of an arrogantly affluent culture that is utterly devoid of social conscience. Amos delivers his heated denunciation unabashedly as though it were "the Word of the Lord." The Spirit, for some reason, does not censor Amos' angle of vision *en route* to its inclusion in the biblical canon.

One of the glories of the four Gospel writers is that, even at the occasional cost of complete consistency, they present no monochromatic proclamation of the good news of Jesus and the inbreaking reign of God. Whatever else we say about those early Christian preachers, this seems fairly certain: they did *not* attend a common seminary homiletics class, where the crucial requirement for passing the course was "One sermon style fits all."

In the graceful quilting of its various contexts, the scriptural record is itself an eloquent witness to the fact that "revelation" is an interpersonal divine-human project; that "the word of the Lord" is never an abstract edict, but always a rich texture of conversational artistry. The preacher who tries, in the interest of proclaiming the revealed truth of God, to "boil it down" to a straightforward series of supposedly divine pronouncements seriously misrepresents the very "revelation" he or she is attempting so assiduously to honor.

Preachers do *not* honor Scripture by turning its vital, vigorous, sometimes contentious conversations into a solo speech composed of simplistic religious slang or elevated religious jargon. They *do* honor it when, in a process respectfully resonant with the very documents that are sources of their sermons, they bear witness to, and orchestrate scriptural voices in *further* conversation with the voices of those who have gathered to hear the Scriptures preached.

Even though it may be offered through a sermon that is prepared and presented by a single preacher, good preaching does not simply issue reports about God's sacred conversations. Rather, good preaching *engages* listeners as *additional partners* in an already ongoing "Spirited" dialogue. The Word of the Lord is thus not only *transmitted*; it is also *extended* and *enriched* in the reflections, discussions, and actions of the Body of Christ.

Sermons shaped in such a way release an energy in some ways akin to the sparks that animate an enthusiastic game of backyard volleyball. Sermon listeners are not long able to remain as detached, sideline observers of a spectator sport. They are pulled onto the court (almost before they know it). They find themselves mixing it up in the sand and the sweat of the other players—taking part in the back-and-forth of the game. They work hard, have fun, take risks. Most important, they get caught up in a Spirit that bears witness with their spirits, assuring them profoundly that they are an integral and valued part of a sacred communal enterprise.

To speak *for* God, as a preacher, if Scripture is our model, is never to preach *at* people. It is not even primarily to preach *to* them. Preaching involves speaking *with* people and *for* them, and speaking with God on their behalf. (Prayer, we shall later suggest, is not just a preparatory exercise for preaching. The entire practice of preaching is prayer infused. Preaching is a special kind of corporate prayer.)

But how does an ordinary preacher translate such a vision into the task of actual sermon shaping? Sermon preparation is an art—one requiring the ongoing interplay of dogged discipline and creative imagination. No boilerplate can be forged for inspired preaching; no checklist will successfully ensure the dance of the Spirit in any given attempt at sermon conversation. It *is* possible, however, to name the conversation partners that the preacher is always seeking to incorporate into the sacred conversations already going on in the texts of Scripture. This book attempts, through the succeeding sections, to designate and briefly describe those distinctive "voices."

The main intent, however, is to allow readers to listen to the sparkling spiritual interchange that can result when preachers welcome many voices into the sermon conversation.

The way in which we have categorized the sermons reprinted in this volume is to some extent arbitrary. Many of the sermons that give clear voice to the specific personal experiences of their preachers, for example, *also* incorporate the voices of the *congregations* being addressed. They further give voice to pressing issues looming large in the consciousness of contemporary *culture*, and to the voice of the *liturgical setting* for which the sermons were prepared. (The same can be said of the sermons that we have included under the other sections.) This crossover is to be expected. Indeed, this is exactly as it should be. The more elements that are active in any sermon conversation (assuming they are clearly differentiated and artfully interwoven), the richer, more "relevant," and more potentially life-transforming the sermon is likely to be.

Still, for purposes of discernment, it is valuable to discriminate the different voices—to "tune in" on one set at a time (which is not unlike playing with the balance in a sophisticated sound system while listening to the recording of an orchestra). By listening specifically for each voice in turn, both preachers and congregation members can learn how the different voices distinctively sound. All who share in the preaching process can thereby discern more perceptively what they are listening for in sermon conversations. They can begin as well to develop a feel for how sermons may be shaped so that those who gather for worship will sense the energy, join the discussion, and thus find themselves affirmed and challenged as members of the fellowship of faith.

In each of these sermons, the voices in Scripture have exercised a critical influence. That influence, however, is seldom exhibited by constant Scripture reference, extended Scripture quotation, or explicit Scriptural analysis. The role of Scripture in these sermons is like that of a respected senior participant who convenes and sets the tone for a lively conversation: contributing occasionally and significantly, but not dominating the discussion or dictating its every move.

To read these "Sermons That Work" with listening imagination is to hear the witness-bearing power of the Spirit. As in previous annual editions of this volume, half of the sermons come from the worship services of an intensive week-long workshop provided by the Episcopal Evangelism Foundation for fostering Excellence in Preaching among Episcopal seminary students. The other sermons come from preachers in Episcopal parishes across the country who have been recognized for significant homiletical artistry through their participation in the annual Best Sermon Contest, another ministry of the same foundation.

SECTION I

PRESIDING BISHOP EDMOND BROWNING SAYS it succinctly in a sermon that appears in Section II: "There is nothing that happens in the life of a priest that cannot be used to edify others. But there is nothing less edifying than the personal anecdotes of a preacher who believes himself to be exemplary."

This is no abstract injunction. Many congregations are captive audiences to varying forms of pulpit exhibitionism. Preachers have cause for pause before employing "personal material" in their sermons. The challenge is always, as John and Caroline Westerhoff have nicely named it, for the "I" of the preacher to function as the "eye" of the sermon.

The experience of the preacher must be an *icon*, a carefully constructed point of focus that then *transfers* the engaged attention to the grace of which the preacher's experience is a manifestation and a symbol. The difference between an *icon* and an *idol* is simple: In homiletical idolatry, the listener's perception becomes fixated on the preacher's experience without moving *through* and *beyond* it.

The simple distinction between moving through and getting stuck is sobering, because it suggests that homiletical idolatry is not necessarily intentional. *(No* form of idolatry ever is.) Even more disquieting is the realization that detecting homiletical idolatry is not a simple matter. A distracting use of the preacher's experience in a sermon cannot be reliably tested for by simply subjecting the manuscript or the recording to an "*I* count." An extended personal testimony in a sermon may be a spiritually transparent icon—a means of spiritual transformation for those whose attention is drawn to the preacher's personal story. On the other hand, listeners can get sidetracked from proper spiritual focus in a sermon whose preacher never uses the word *I* even once.

Just as there can be no abstract definition of pornography (even though it can often be readily recognized), so there are no absolute defining rules for ensuring idolatry avoidance in a sermon. Negative example is never the most effective means of instruction. What follows in this section of the book, therefore, is a series of positive examples. In each sermon, the point of departure, the angle of interpretive vision, or the issue of spiritual concern is generated by an experience that the preacher has previously undergone firsthand. The listener's ear is attracted to the voice of the preacher's experience without being mesmerized.

To attract such healthy attention, it is not necessary for the preacher to recount a dramatic personal story (although, as will shortly be evident, such strategies are not *precluded*.)

Roger Alling's sermon was the opening event of the 1996 Preaching Excellence Program, held at Capital University in Columbus, Ohio. Alling draws on the memory of an utterly nondramatic family situation with which he "grew up" in order to provide a point of entry for considering an appointed Evensong lesson from Ephesians. The icon of Alling's experience makes the Scripture immediately relevant for fledgling preachers at the outset of an exciting, but potentially threatening, conference week.

It is an experience later in life, while a student in seminary, that provides **Linda Clader** with an icon of her own spiritual journey and a means of inviting her listeners into a similarly risky religious adventure. A prison cell—experienced "up close and personal"—is the springboard for a sympathetic reappraisal of poor old tradition-bound St. Peter. It also graphically poses a challenge for sermon listeners to take "freedom in Christ" as something more than an abstract theological assertion.

The extended experiences of a much subtler and more pervasive social-cultural incarceration gives **Eugene Sutton** the impetus for rigorously questioning a common, innocent-sounding interpretation of a familiar Gospel text. After hearing Sutton preach on what is involved for Jesus in "honoring the child," it is unlikely that careful listeners will ever again be tempted to smile and say of Jesus' references to children: "Isn't that sweet?"

Rick Oberheide's personal experience is dramatic. A clear crisis point for the preacher becomes a striking and unusual turning point in a sermon on unity. Without becoming sensationalistic, his "Easter experience" snaps listeners into full alert before they doze off, expecting one more earnest moral exhortation to "just be nice" in the face of serious community conflict.

Anne Bartlett does not so much *give* her "personal testimony" as *use* it. A "moment of truth" in her life becomes a homiletical hologram for interweaving similar moments in the lives of Jesus' disciples—those disciples being described in the Gospel text itself and those disciples being addressed *by* the sermon shaped *from* the text.

What evokes the song of the Spirit in the Scripture texts of these sermons? What serves as a lead-in to the broad cultural issues and the specific congregational concerns that each sermon addresses? It is the word of the Lord that each preacher has heard in the distinctive particularity of his or her own experience. The "*I*" of the preacher becomes the "eye" of the sermon through which we can look—upon Scripture, ourselves, each other—and toward God.

Preachers Who Have to Say Something and Preachers Who Have Something to Say
A Sermon at Evening Prayer
The Preaching Excellence Program, 1996
by Roger Alling

Propers: Ecclesiasticus 42:15-25 and Ephesians 3:14-21

∞

Caesar said, "All Gaul is divided into three parts," but more to our purposes this week is the truth that all preachers are divided into two groups: Those who have to say something and those who have something to say.

This was one of my father's favorite one line jokes about preachers; he was a preacher himself. As a teenage listener at midday Sunday dinner I used to ask myself silently about my father: Did he have to say something this morning, or did he really have something to say?

My father was not a great preacher. His great gift for ministry was as pastor. He worked at preaching as hard as anyone I have ever known. He put in the time and the effort, and he knew how important the preaching task was.

The results were a mixed bag. Sometimes he would have a so-so inning in the pulpit—not great, but not bad. Other times he would swing and dribble one outside the third base line, to his and others' disappointment. But every now and then Dad would lean back, step into the pulpit, and put one out of the bleachers for a real grand slam.

I wondered for years what made the difference. I asked myself what it was like to preach and what went into the process that produced the event of preaching and listening in church that took place each week. I have been fascinated with this process ever since.

What about you? Where are you in the preaching spectrum? Do you already have a real sense of what you feel called to say and how to go about saying it? Or are you full of fear and trembling at the prospect of getting into the pulpit forty or so times a year to proclaim a word from God to those committed to your charge?

All of us are at at either of these places from time to time. There will be those Sundays when you can't wait to finish the gospel reading so that you can have your say, and other Sundays when the prospect of standing up to preach will seem to be more than you can face. As one preacher who has experienced these feelings many times, I can only say on reflection that I feel better now about those times when I was anxious about getting into the pulpit than I do about some of those times when I entered the pulpit a bit too full of a confidence sadly misplaced.

Some of you may have heard the story of the new deacon who preached at a festival service in the presence of the bishop. At the end of the sermon the new deacon misspoke and said loudly, "This is the Gospel of the Lord," at which point the bishop was heard to say under his breath, "I seriously doubt it!"

I remember the time when a member of the youth group of our parish asked me, one Sunday evening, whether it made me nervous to face the congregation each week in the pulpit. "Aren't you worried that the people might not like what you say to them?" I acknowledged that peoples' reactions concerned me somewhat but then went on to say that my real prayer was that what I said in the pulpit would be found acceptable to God and be at least somewhat faithful to the Gospel.

As you think about preaching, which makes you more nervous? Is it the reaction of your congregation week by week, or the nagging worry that you'll get the gospel wrong and misrepresent it in your preaching? There is nothing new about these worries. They have been around since the beginning.

The section of the letter to the Ephesians we read this evening is addressed to nervous preachers who worry about their audiences and what they will say to them.

Earlier in this chapter, Paul, or his stand-in, tells what it means for him to be a preacher. "To me, though I am the very least of all the saints, this grace was given, to preach to the Gentiles the unsearchable riches of Christ, and to make all people see what is the plan of the mystery hidden for ages in God who created all things. . ."

Just think for a moment about Paul's understanding of his vocation. Aware of his limitations, relying only on God's grace, he is to preach to the Gentiles so that all people will be able to see God's mystery and plan for the creation. The goal Paul sets for preaching is huge. All people are to be made able to see the whole of God's mystery and plan from the Creation to the Eschaton.

How do you prepare for a preaching ministry this large? Only God can make it possible, so Paul prays for us and for all who would be preachers of the Gospel. Hear him once more:

*For this reason I bow my knee before the Father, . . . that he may grant
you to be strengthened with might through his Spirit in the inner man,*

and that Christ may dwell in your hearts through faith; that you may have power to comprehend with all the saints what is the breadth and length and height and depth . . . to know the love of Christ which surpasses knowledge, that you may be filled with all the fullness of God.

The journey to become a preacher begins inside. You cannot share what you do not have. The unsearchable riches of Christ must be in your heart before you can help plant them in someone else through your words and through your preaching.

In his translation of Ephesians 3, Markus Barth capitalizes *Inner Man* and suggests that the Inner Man of this passage is none other than the Christ who dwells in us. Barth understands the Inner Man as being the reality of the unity Christ has with each of us, the unity we have with each other, the unity that exists in our communities, and the unity that exists between the preachers and those who hear them.

The goal of our preaching is not something that we give and others receive. The goal of our preaching is something that we come to share. It is a comprehension of the love and goodness of God, which can only be had with all the saints. It is born of a love that surpasses mere knowledge and is a comprehension able to fill us with all the fullness of God.

Have you ever noticed that the sermon is never over until it has been preached? All the preparation in the world does not make the sermon. The sermon is only the sermon when it has been preached and heard in the fellowship of the faithful. "How did it go today?" is never just a question about the preacher's work or her performance. *How it went* as an event in the life of God's church is the real question and the question that counts the most. The sermon "works" only if the saints are able to comprehend together a portion of the manifest fullness of God.

By herself or himself an ordained person may not celebrate the Eucharist. By himself or herself a preacher does not make a sermon.

Our Foundation puts on this annual Preaching Excellence Program because we care about the preaching task. We care about those of us who are called to preach and for all of us who are called to comprehend the mystery hidden through the ages in God.

We are delighted that you are here and confident that the time spent this week will be useful for those who believe we have something to say and for those who only know now that we will someday have to say something.

Prison Cells

The Rev. Linda L. Clader
The Preaching Excellence Program 1996

Galatians 2:11-21

∞

His name was the Duke—or at least that's what they called him—
    he had a face like a Christmas-card cherub
    and he played the piano like a bat out of hell—
    jazz, blues, and on Sundays—
        on Sundays with his piano he led the Gospel Choir.
I'm not sure what he was in for,
    but while I was doing my time in CPE, the Duke was paroled.
I remember his last day around the prison chapel.
    Applause for him, handshakes and hugs — and some tears —
    best wishes, all around.
    On Monday, the Duke was on the bus for Oakland.
And pretty soon, I was out of prison, too, back to seminary for my
    last year.

Now, I'd had such a good time doing CPE at the state prison,
    that my last semester I finagled a reading course
    that took me back to prison again as a volunteer chaplain.
And when I went into the chapel on my first day back,
    there, pounding away on a gospel hymn, was the Duke.
His friends were all around him, singing those gospel hymns.
And while he played, his face was lit up in a beatific grin,
    just like a Christmas card angel.
It sure looked like he was glad to be back home.

We all know the stories of how people become "convicts"—
    so used to the control over their lives,
    so comfortable with the rigidity, the daily regimen,
    so secure in the limits imposed on them,
    that they become incapable of living free anymore,
    incapable of surviving on the outside,
    at a loss about how to make their way amid so much flexibility,
    so much freedom, so much uncertainty.

When you're in a situation where you're firmly controlled,
    where your every move is programmed,
    you can start to feel as if you have the control—
life is predictable—an action has a definite reaction—
    it feels secure, even when the security is imposed from outside.
So it broke my heart to see him back inside there—
    Duke, the piano player with the face of an angel—
It broke my heart, but it didn't surprise me.

Now, I think all of us can understand something about this.
    We're just going along, living our little lives,
    in a familiar, predictable, well-defined pattern, and something
    happens—a chance encounter—a personal tragedy—or a success—
    or the voice of God—something happens that calls us to step outside.
    Something makes it clear to us that it's time to go on a quest—an
    adventure—to grow up—or to cross a threshold—
    to turn in another direction—to take a new path—
Something cracks open a door and the light shines in,
    and we glimpse brighter colors on the other side of the door.
And we stretch our arms, and take a deep breath, and those shackles
    fall off, and we march out the door—into the air and the light and
    the freedom—
And we're way out here with no boundaries—no patterns—
no structures—
    NO BOUNDARIES! NO PATTERNS! NO STRUCTURES!
    NOTHING TO HANG ONTO!
    None of the old ways of knowing for sure who you are—
And you look around frantically, and you start to shake,
and that old prison cell, that old life starts to look real good.
And the demons and the monsters who dwell at the thresholds
    of the gates that lead to new life—
those demons and monsters start whispering,
    "Go back! Go back where it's safe! Go back where you know
    who you are!
    Go back, or we'll eat you alive!"
It's sure tempting, in the face of the fearful chaos of it all,
    it's sure tempting to find a way to violate your parole,
    and get sent back to those cinder block walls,
    where you can count on three square meals and a bed.
Even when we've glimpsed freedom, even when we've had a taste of
real life, It's easy to want to return to what's known,

what's dependable, what's certain.

Which is why I hope we can find it in our hearts to cut old St. Peter a
little slack,
    for blowing it again, under pressure,
    and turning away from sharing a meal with Gentiles.
I think we Christians are so familiar with Paul's side of this,
    the wonderful good news that the doors of salvation
        have been opened not only to the Jews
        but to the Gentiles (that's us, of course).
We're all so familiar with Paul's "Law versus Grace" opposition
    that we forget how incredibly hard it had to be
    for a Jew to walk through that door
    out of the constraints of the Law into the bright, colorful new life
    in Christ, and into a dinner party—full of Gentiles!
Think how that must have been!

Now, I'd like you to fold your hands. Notice which thumb is on top.
Now fold them with the other thumb on top. And for the next week,
I want you to do it this way, every time. See how easy it is.

Now, here we all sit, preachers of the Good News,
    called by Jesus Christ to proclaim release to the captives.
And the walls and the iron gates that imprison the people of this land
    are easy enough for us to see.
We can see our neighbors imprisoned by the myth of success—
    "If you only work your heart out, you, too, can achieve
    the dream."
And we can see them imprisoned by their fear of each other,
    fear of intimacy, fear of violence, which is ultimately their
    fear of death.
And we can see them imprisoned by that terror that lies underneath
    all fears—the fear that none of this, life or death, has any meaning.
But the old stories and the old fears have become so familiar to them
    that their prison has become home,
    and the promise of freedom in Christ, of life in Christ,
    feels like the threat of a great loss, feels like a vision of the abyss.

This is what we're dealing with, when we try to call people to a life
    of faith.
Although people will say they want freedom,

you punch a homiletical hole in that prison wall
and before you can say "theotokos,"
they'll be hauling bricks and mortar to plug it up again.
It's human nature.
It's our nature, too.

Which is, exactly, the point.
Before we get too frustrated with a world that refuses to hear
    our well-tuned proclamation,
Before we become cynical
    about the stubbornness of people who keep building their
    own prisons,
We need to pray the Holy Spirit to guide us—us preachers, us priests—
    to recognize the prison cells we build for ourselves.
Where are the hidden places, the secure places,
    where we retreat to find certainty,
    when we get scared of having too much freedom?
Where are the cells where we can feel in control
    in the face of too much mystery?
Do we build those high-security cells out of a theology that asks no
    questions?
Do we build them out of nervousness that the Bible can't
    stand criticism,
    or that Jesus is too holy to argue with, man to man?
Do we build them out of reliance on the centuries of privilege
    that we Anglicans have come to expect, to depend on,
    even when we joke about it?
Do we build them out of the unspoken fear that if we lose the favor
    of the powerful, we'll discover that our faith was grounded on
    nothing, after all?

If we are going to take a captive by the hand,
    and draw her with us into the light of Christ,
We need to be in touch—regularly, always—
    with our own fears, with our own knee-jerk urges
    to retreat into our own prison cells.
And because it's very hard to make out the shape of our own walls,
    our own cells, since we've got them painted nice and decorated
    with posters or banners, and maybe lit with candles and smoked
    up with incense,
because our own prison walls are so hard to see,

we need to pray, unceasingly—with our hands folded this new
    way—that the Holy Spirit will move somebody to preach to us—
    to knock out our walls.
We need to pray, unceasingly,
    that the Holy Spirit will use a crowbar, if necessary,
    to pry open our hearts to the mystery,
    to the uncertain, to the unmanageability of God's grace.
That, brother and sister preachers, takes what Paul calls faith.
The kind of faith that Jesus had.
The kind of radical, all-the-way-open faith
    that leads out of prisons into freedom.
The kind of faith that leads to death, and to resurrection.

"I have been crucified with Christ;
    and it is no longer I who live,
    but it is Christ who lives in me.
And the life I now live in the flesh
    I live by faith in the Son of God,
    by the faith of the Son of God,
    who loved me, and gave himself for me."

That kind of faith.

Nobodies

Eugene Taylor Sutton
Chaplain of the Diocese of New Jersey,
Adjunct Professor of Homiletics at the
General Theological Seminary

∞

"...On the way they had argued with one another who was the greatest."
(Mark 9:34)

When I was growing up in Washington, D.C., a local automobile dealer aired a series of television commercials that captured the fancy of the entire metropolitan area. Against a stark black backdrop without music or fanfare, the scene showed the middle-aged dealer sitting alone, staring into the camera, and then finally saying in a slow, deep voice the following words:

> *Nobody* can sell you a car like I can.
> *Nobody* can make you a better deal than me.
> *Noooooo...body!*

Those words really grabbed me and my friends. I remember for months on end we would "shoot the dozens"—street slang for the fine art of the insult-capping our elaborate put-downs with the exquisitely phrased "Noooooo ... body!" Not only would we make fun of each other, but we took special delight in verbally abusing the "point-two's" in our communities—the bums, drug addicts, hobos, panhandlers, and other street people—so-called because we read somewhere that there were 3.2 persons in the average American family. They were the ".2" people, the *real* nobodies.

Why did that word so grip our imaginations? Not just because we were preadolescent kids, in a stage of life known for its fascination with cruelty. Rather, I think we resonated with the word because we knew deep down in our souls that *we* were nobodies, and we knew that because society treated us as though we were nobodies. You know our nation's capital, don't you? Not the "official" Washington of beautiful parks and monuments, but the "other" city that is predominantly black, many of whose people are trapped in desperate poverty. Not too long ago the city was known as the murder capital of the world, with its several drug-infested and crime-ridden neighborhoods giving up a slain young black male on a daily basis.

We were nobodies. Many of our parents had no-good jobs. Many of us lived in no-good housing. We attended no-good schools. Sometimes we would take the bus to go downtown where the really important people were—the *somebodies*—who didn't look like us. They certainly didn't live where we lived. When I was about four years old, I remember moving into a neighborhood where my family were the only African Americans. Within a few years all of the white families had moved away, with all their kids whom I had become friends with. Even at that young age I received the message that I was considered a nobody, because the people who mattered in society did not want to live next to me, or my family, or my people.

So, let's add it up: no-good neighbors leads to no-good city services and schools, leading to no-good education, leading to no-good jobs, leading to ".2 s", resulting in an environment of "nobodyness." Society was telling me that *I* was a nobody. And so was my father. And so was my mother.

It's through that lens that I read today's gospel lesson of Mark 9:33-37, particularly verse 35, *"Whoever wants to be first must be last of all and servant of all."* Was Jesus for real? Did he have the "nobodies" of the world in mind when he said this? Jesus made the statement in response to his disciples arguing with one another who was the greatest. Isn't it natural that those on the bottom rungs of the social ladder will strive and desire for the top rung? One of our heroes growing up was the heavyweight boxing champion Muhammad Ali, boldly announcing to the world, "I'm the greatest!" The desire to be that is a universal sentiment—to be the greatest nation, the greatest power in the world, the greatest city, the greatest neighborhood in that city; to belong to the greatest church, and to be known as the greatest preacher in that church . . . or maybe just to give the greatest sermon at the Episcopal Preaching Excellence Program? You get the point. Acting out of some sense of "nobodies" deeply imbedded in our lives, we all at some time covet the imaginary title of "greatest," or we want to be associated with it. Whether we were raised in Washington, D.C., or Palm Beach, Florida, the Bronx or the Upper East Side, in Watts or on Wilshire Boulevard, we are all the same: no one wants to be last, everyone strives to be the greatest. And we believe that greatness is measured by strength, military might, wealth, fame, social prestige, or any other conventional standard of power.

But Jesus pointed the way out of the desperate need to achieve an elusive "greatness"—a "chasing after wind" (Ecclesiastes 1:17). He took into his arms a little child, identifying himself not with power, but vulnerability. His lifting up the child as an example was in marked contrast to the low esteem in which children were held in Greco-Roman society; indeed, the word used for "child" in this passage is the same word used for the Suffering Servant of the Lord in the Greek version of Isaiah 53:2, "We heralded him as a child." By embracing the child, Jesus identified himself with the lowliest, the least, and the servant of all.

The answer in Mark's Gospel to the unhealthy striving after greatness is not an exhortation to be like a child, that is, to "be humble!" and thereby work harder than anyone else to be known as "the greatest humble person" in your community. In Alan Paton's book, *Instrument of Thy Peace*, he tells of a rabbi, a cantor, and a humble synagogue cleaner who are preparing for the Day of Atonement. The rabbi beat his breast, and said: "I am nothing. I am nothing." The cantor beat his breast, and said: "I am nothing. I am nothing." The cleaner beat his breast, and said: "I am nothing. I am nothing." And the rabbi said to the cantor: "Look who thinks *he's* nothing!"

Instead of making the work of humility another virtue to be achieved, Jesus in today's Gospel reading says, "Receive (welcome) the child in my name." Or, in other words, "Welcome your true humanity before God. Welcome your inability to reach the world's unhealthy and destructive standards of greatness. Don't be so hard on yourself; remember that you are a child of God, so welcome the child. By welcoming your own vulnerability, your 'nobodyness,' you are welcoming *me*."

There is an old African American spiritual that I learned as a child in church:

> *Nobody knows the trouble I see,*
> *Nobody knows my sorrow.*
> *Nobody knows the trouble I see,*
> *Glory, Halleluia!*

I always wondered how my African forbears could sing of all their troubles that nobody knows or even cares about, and then end with the doxology, "Glory, Halleluia!" But now I've come to appreciate the profound theological wisdom of the spiritual, especially when it comes to the last refrain:

> *Nobody knows the trouble I see*
> *Nobody knows . . . but Jesus!*

That's right! Nobody knows the troubles, the sorrows, the injustices of the world as God knows incarnate in Jesus—the supreme "Nobody" whom the world rejected. When Jesus was falsely arrested on trumped up charges, inadequately represented in a mockery of a trial, and finally executed by a corrupt state interested only in eliminating perceived threats to its religious, social, and political power, he had—

> *No money*
> *No social standing*
> *No following willing to stand up for him*
> *No decent funeral or burial*
> *Nobody.*

Jesus was nobody. Just like my childhood friends and me, among a nobody people. God incarnate made a choice to identify with the nobodies of the world . . . Glory, Halleluia!

So, what are you going to do? Well, you're going to have to make a decision. You may decide to *follow* Jesus on the way to his crucifixion and resurrection. If so, you must "welcome the child," accepting your own lowliness and vulnerability as well as learning to live with the nobodies whom Jesus loved and identified with. This choice may not get you much of the world's success that you might otherwise achieve, but you will have the joy that comes only from being in fellowship with God. As the Anglican poet Thomas Traherne once wrote, "Til you can sing and rejoice and delight in God, as misers do in gold, and Kings in scepters, you will never enjoy the world."

Or you may decide *not to follow Jesus*, probably because having the comforts and esteem associated with "greatness" is too important for you. If you decide this, you may still be known as a "good" Christian—you may even do well in ministry and be quite successful. But one night you will not be able to sleep, for you will look at your life and all that you have accumulated and feel that it all didn't matter. You would have gladly given it all away for the surpassing worth of being in close communion with Jesus as he went along his way. But you chose to go another path, leaving him behind.

Welcome the child . . . embrace the child . . . receive the child!

Easter in the Emergency Room

Rick Oberheide
McChord AFB Chapel
Easter 7

John 17: 20-26

∞

I well remember my first "war" on the battlefield of ministry. It was over the color of new carpet for the church. One group wanted dark brown, the other wanted a lighter tan. I was young, new to the parish ministry, and utterly bewildered by the intensity of the war that raged around me. I was well aware that conflict was written on every page of church history, but I'd never been caught so intensely in the middle of it. Those were also the days when pitched battles over the Prayer Book and women's ordination were being fought. My own church was thus divided over carpet, the diocese over liturgy and gender. The church then seemed like anything *but* a place of unity or oneness in Christ. In some ways, it still doesn't.

We need to listen closely to Jesus' prayer for unity in the Gospel of John. First, a quick look at what he is praying for. He is praying for those who believe, with no distinction between believers then and now. He is praying for us, that we all may be one. Just as he is one with God, we are to be one with him and God. Then, because we are one with God and Christ, the world will believe. What we have in that is a simple, neat, theological formula: A + B = C. (A: his unity with God + B: our unity in him = C: the world believes). And what in the world does all that mean to embattled, divided churches?

The foundation and hope of his prayer rest in his claim, "I and the Father are one." Who he claims to be represents the focus and means of all Christian unity. His claim of oneness with God often passes over heads in the form of theological or creedal language, in such words as: "very God of very God, begotten not made . . . of one being with the Father . . . God from God, light from light." We say and hear these words weekly. I wonder how often we thoughtlessly say the words, never fully considering what such language represents.

We need to translate the lofty, theological words of our formal beliefs into the everyday language of time, place, and person. What Jesus' claim of oneness with God says in historical terms is this: a sweaty, first-century carpenter was *God*. The claim of the creeds in plain language is that a 30- to 33-year-old itinerant preacher who was beaten and hanged naked between two common criminals *was the Alpha and the Omega*. What we are saying in the Easter proclamation is that his resurrection *really happened*. We are saying in the most historical terms that the source of all life and creation transformed a broken, dead body back to life. To put all of that historical language into present-day terms, we are claiming that the same power present in the moment of resurrection is available to us—this moment. We are saying that Jesus, today, is the source of healing, change, transformation.

There is nothing distant or mystical about such claims. And there are only two possibilities for us to consider regarding the life and claims of Jesus. The first is that he was totally insane, the David Koresh of his day. In psychiatric terms, he suffered from some delusional disorder that manifested itself in confusing himself with God. Somehow, his followers bought into the delusion, wrote it all down, and here we are today shopping for carpet. If that is our belief, then let us live unto the world, fill our storehouses, stay in control, live unto self, win at all costs. If Jesus wasn't one with the Father, then the bumper sticker is correct: He who dies with the most toys, wins. If Jesus isn't who he said, then let us periodically mumble religious language without thought or commitment, and let church be nothing more than another item on our social checklist.

The other possibility for our consideration is that Jesus' words are factually, historically true: He is the Son of God, the source of all life, healing, hope, salvation. It is precisely such belief that is at the core of who we *are* and what we *proclaim* as the church. Such active belief is at the core of his word for us: believers. It is the belief that Jesus is the Son of the living God that is the very source of any shred of unity we share. We are not, in such terms, theologians who debate the nature of God; we are rather proclaimers who share the good news of God among us, as such news is revealed by Scripture.

I wasn't thinking much about such issues or claims this past Easter morning, when I suddenly found myself at death's door. I expected that morning to preach and celebrate the reality of Easter. I did not expect to experience Good Friday in the form of terrible pain brought on by a 100 percent blocked artery; the fearful, lonely realization in the ambulance that I might be in the process of dying, the chaos and humiliation of having my clothes cut off, then lying naked in the midst of a dozen or so strangers in the emergency room. It was my darkest, most lonely hour. The thief in the night, suddenly and unexpectedly there at *my* door. I felt afraid, alone, and totally out of control. In the midst of that personal Good Friday, Easter was proclaimed to me when one of the emergency room technicians bent down over my face with a bright, happy smile and loudly said: "Happy Easter!" What he said to me in those two words was this: "You may live, you may die; in either case, Christ is risen!" His was a wonderfully bold and simple sermon; the best I'd every heard, and one I will never forget.

We, as the Body of Christ, need to continue saying and listening to Jesus' prayer for unity. The church, obviously, remains divided in many ways and places. We are divided today over issues: homosexuality, abortion, the death penalty. We square off over matters of liturgy and style. Building programs can become ugly power struggles, and the fighting is not always fair. Individuals leave churches in a huff over matters as trivial as the color of carpeting or the length of candles. Whole denominations split acrimoniously over issues of biblical interpretation.

The seeming assumption of the *church* in such matters is that once we settle matters of doctrine, social obligation, and liturgy we will then achieve the unity Jesus prays for. The idea is that once we "get it right," we will then be one in Christ. So "this group" squares off against "that group" in a game of ecclesiastical capture-the-flag. The focus and politics of the church are then lived out in terms of a mad scramble to get to the top of the hill, upon which "I am right and you are wrong." All of which puts the cart before the horse.

The truth is that we can share oneness only as we surrender our lives to Christ, *at the bottom of the hill,* from where we look up to him. Such collective surrender, based on our shared belief that *he is who he says he is,* is the foundation of a unified church. It is impossible to look down on anyone when together we look up to Christ, united by our brokenness as people and our belief that he is God. In the context of such shared belief, different styles of worship are no more important than different colors of hair. When unified by shared surrender to Christ's lordship, members of different denominations are no longer suspicious strangers or total enemies; they are more like different vegetables sharing the same bowl—each bringing different flavors and nutrients to a hungry world.

Unity does not, in such terms, mean uniformity. Differences are allowed, encouraged, and—when necessary—negotiated in love. Neither does unity mean the absence of conflict or acrimony.

Passionate belief often demands intense conflict. When we get to heaven we will receive the final answers to current matters of raging debate. We hope that in the midst of passionate dispute, the world will not see and define us by our battles and divisions. We hope and pray that until we get to heaven, the world will hear loudest and clearest our proclamation that Jesus is Lord, and that apart from him we are hopelessly lost. Those are matters of life and death that must define everything we say and do as the church.

Our proclamation today is *nothing* less than this: Jesus Christ is the Son of God, the very source of our now and our forever. May we as the Body of Christ joyfully smile into the eyes of a society dying in the emergency room, and let us boldly proclaim through the sacraments, our lives, and our shared ministry: "Happy Easter!"

But Who Do You Say That I Am?

The Rev. Anne K. Bartlett
Associate Rector, Parish of St. John the Baptist
Portland, Oregon

Friday of Week Two	*Isaiah 53:11-12*
Proposed Daily Eucharistic Lectionary	*Psalm 66:1-11*
The Preaching Excellence Program, 1996	*Luke 9:18-26*
Columbus, Ohio	

∞

May the words of my mouth and the meditation of my heart be always acceptable in thy sight, O Lord, my strength and my redeemer. Amen.

Though it has been twenty-odd years, I remember as if it were last week the first time I really and truly heard the question. I was in my usual spot—Gospel side, two-thirds of the way back, left shoulder against the end of the pew—safe (or so I thought). In his usual spot was the priest, Charlie (whom I trusted—and I didn't trust many in those days), reading in his everyday voice the terrifying, wondrous Gospel words. I'm sure I had heard them before, but I could not tell you when. Forever in my memory, I hear the question as on the day I first heard it, summer sunshine filtering through the vertical slit of the simple stained glass window, scattering geometric pieces of blue light like jewels onto the red carpet and across Charlie's white alb, the shapes and colors like a child's work of art. The Gospel book gleamed with a light of its own as I heard the eternal question of our Christian faith: "But who do you say that I am?"

Where were you when you were first fully confronted with those words?

I did not know it then, of course, but now it seems to me quite clear that the impact of that question hit me at a crossroad of my life and turned me around and set me along the way that brought me here, brought all of us here, to this point, this place this morning, as we wend our way home. The question is the question of the Christian life and, quite specifically, the question of those of us who are called to the preaching life.

It is not, however, the first question Our Lord asked his disciples that day. The first question is much easier. Once, on one fine day, out of the blue (as Luke tells the story), Jesus was praying alone, the rest of the group nearby . . . wait a minute. Freeze-frame. What were they doing, Peter and James and Joanna, Matthew, Mary, Susanna, and Andrew? I assume it is morning, but there is nothing in the text to support such a claim. So, there, in the morning light . . . wait again. Which morning is it? The morning in my memory when I first heard this text? Or the morning on which Our Lord asked his question of his first disciples? Or does it matter? (For me, it is in the holographic morning light that I slip into the text, but perhaps for you it is late afternoon.) There is Jesus, a little way off, in prayer, and the rest of us are mingling about the campsite. I seem to have a cup of coffee in my hands with my back to the others, and I am staring off into the middle distance, half in daydream and still trying to wrap my mind about what happened a week or so ago when we fed thousands upon thousands of men and women and children with five loaves of bread and two fish. I turn when I hear my Master's voice asking (in what kind of tone? Bemused, I think; perhaps a little curious, even): "Who do the crowds say that I am? What are others saying about me?"

Ah, that question we can answer. "Well," we say, "the word on the street is this: Back then, some thought you were John the Baptist, or Elijah, or a reincarnation of an ancient prophet come back to earth. Today, two thousand years later, the word from the seminars is this: You were a typical Jewish peasant, and others say you were a rabbinnical wisdom teacher or maybe a member of the Essene sect, and a lot of scholars writing best-sellers are saying they are sure you never said or did most of what we thought you said and did and maybe were not who we thought you were." On and on we glibly talk about who the others say he is.

Our Lord soon loses patience with that conversation. He said to them, he says to us: "But who do you say that I am?" And there I am again, twenty-some-odd years ago, on that summer Sunday when the blue shards of light splattered over Charlie's alb, and my heart broke, and my Lord's question dropped in.

Here's the way I see it: Those of us who are preachers are forever at that campsite, mingling about the fire in the foggy early light, spending more time than we admit (though in many ways it is the most important time we spend), staring off into the middle distance, coffee cups in hand, half in daydream as we ponder the mysteries of the journey and the wonders of the Way, Our Lord's question ever hanging in the air: "But who do you say that I am?"

When I'm afflicted with self-consciousness or separated from my own true self or riddled with self-doubt, that is when I am tempted to preach an answer to his first-asked question—to talk about what others say about him. And is that not how we are trained? To exegete, to locate in historical time and space, to use the best of our tradition and the insights of our saints and scholars? You bet that's how we are to prepare to preach; it is our bounden duty and service, and rightly so. Our sermons will soon show if we are not thus grounded. But it is not enough, of course. Oh, we might get by for a year or two or ten, but our talk will soon wear thin if all we have to say is what "the others" think.

"But who do you say that I am?" "You are the Christ." The question has come to all of us, or we would not be here. It's that simple. The details of our experiences—when we first truly heard the question and whispered back, "You are the Christ"—the details are as unique to us as our own fingerprints, but on them all is visible the fingerprint of God. At some crossroad along the way we were turned and chose to spend our lives struggling with, delighting in, suffering the question. The Christian preaching life is to wrestle with the paradox of the Word made flesh, the attendant ambiguities, with our own ambivalences, humbled with the inconsistencies of our response. How well we know that it is through grace alone that we, with Peter, dare to say out loud, "You are the Christ." And even when we, full of grace, can so proclaim, we still don't understand what it is we have just said. The mystery is beyond us, always, this side of the kingdom. Then there is this: As soon as we blurt out who we think He is, then we find that our old answers to who we think we are no longer hold.

I have a friend who is pastor of a large Presbyterian congregation, a flaming red-haired woman named Heidi who stands over six feet tall, freckle-faced, strong-boned, self-assured, with a deserved reputation for being a powerful preacher. Five of us meet monthly to mingle, and to muse, and to talk about how the journey goes. Last time we spoke of preaching. The conversation deepened, slowed, became more hesitant and tender. Then Heidi said, "Every time . . . every time I climb into the pulpit I hear this little voice in the back of my head whispering, 'Who do you think you are? Who do you think you are to preach to these people? Why should they listen to you?'"

That question has a real hook. If we would live our lives answering out loud the question of who we say He is, then we must struggle, too, with who it is we think we are when we dare to preach. We know—I pray to God we know—that every time we preach there will be in the congregation those who have more active prayer lives, those who have more insights, those who live more faithful lives of service, those who know and yes, love Jesus better than we do. My beloved colleague tells the story of when he was a young priest and Sister Mary Anselm, a religious giant now gone to glory, asked him to be her spiritual director. He said, "Oh, I can't." She said, "I know." And they went on from there, for more than twenty-five years.

Who do we think we preachers think we are? We say we can't and God says "I know," and we go on from there. The voice in Heidi's head and in your head and in my head, when it is of God, tempers our pride and puts us in our proper place before God and with our people. The voice is not of God, however, when it makes us mute, holds us back from that which is our joy and work to do: to find our voices, to speak out loud, to dare to witness to the One whom we call Lord, preaching with passion and with energy and in words upon which this desperately hungry world of ours can feed. If we say he is the Christ, that he is the Word made flesh, then we also say that we are flesh made Word when we are graced to preach like that.

There is a price, of course. When we offer up our souls and bodies to become flesh-made-Word, then we give up ourselves. We make the turning at the crossroads, we follow where the truth may lead, and we lose pieces of our selves along the way. The losses are real. Let's be clear about that. But it is mostly our false selves that daily die—those shiny little armored pieces we wear on the outside of our souls. That question—"Who do you think you are, to be a preacher of the Word?"—is of God when it comes not as our accuser but as life-transforming cross, forming Christ more and more within us as the false self dies. Our true self is then freed to be an open-throated channel through which the Spirit might speak.

I don't know how to put the process more plainly. I can only tell you how this preaching life is for me. The truth of my life is that God made me a preacher because that is how God saves me. At heart, I think that's why any of us get to preach, are allowed to be priests. It's not about what gifts we may give to others—that's gravy. If through our preaching God's word is spoken, if we become for a moment "flesh made Word," that is God's gift to us.

Somehow, somewhere, we heard the question, it fell into our broken hearts one ordinary day, one fine day, and then the really interesting part of our lives began. And here we are, and here we've been for this extraordinary, grace-filled week of hearing the Word, of feasting upon the Word, of daring to speak to one another of the truths we think we know about the Word, and all the while the sun has scattered divine light and energy among us like jewels. We leave bespattered with the light as if we were a work of children's art. And now we preachers, we lovers of words, we lovers of the Word, we take pieces of each other as we go and leave pieces of ourselves behind, giving thanks to God for this precious time, this holy campsite where we mingled around the holy fire and played with holy words and where we are now graced to gather round this holy table in the morning light. Oh, dear friends. How wondrous is our God to call us—even us—to such a life of grace.

Amen.

"I Have Heard the Cry of My People"
The Voice of the Spirit in the Life of the Congregation

HOW FAVORABLY DO YOU RESPOND WHEN A LETTER BEGINS: "To Whom It May Concern," "Dear Friend," or "Dear Mr. and Mrs. Sullivan" (if you are, in fact, an avowedly single Ms. Sullivan)? The feeling inside, upon receiving such a letter, is probably like the feeling you have if an office-seeking politician takes you by the hand, looks you straight in the eye, and yet is clearly seeing not you, but "The Public." In such situations we are not really addressed. We may feel ignored, slighted, even insulted.

Clutching theological preconceptions about "the human condition," and "God's unchanging Truth," preachers often try to peddle universal spiritual principles in their sermons, principles that sound in the ears of listeners like nothing more than empty generic platitudes. Even tender invitations to "a personal relationship with Jesus" can easily come across to hungry, hurting individuals as though they were mass-produced, sentimental Hallmark cards bedecked with hearts and roses, inscribed with "Be My Valentine."

In facing any congregation, a preacher confronts an enormous challenge: to establish an authentic spiritual connection that is genuinely personal, *without* transgressing any listener's private space. How to do this—for all assembled?

Equal time for all congregants, of course, is not only impossible but ill-advised. No congregation has enough interest or patience to endure the parade, across a single sermon stage, of every conceivable variant in the human situation. And yet, the preacher who addresses the concerns of "everyone" in all likelihood will make connection with *no one*.

The challenge for the preacher is actually much larger than simply that of a speaker trying to "pitch" a talk to a particular audience. The Spirit speaks *through* as well as *to* the particular circumstances and concerns of any given congregation. As we suggested earlier, preaching involves speaking *with* and *for* the listeners as much as—or more than—speaking *to* them.

This extra burden on the preacher, however, usually turns out to have a blessing attached. As they listen to the Scriptures through the ears of distinctive constituencies, and as they try to voice the good news in ways that are authentic to their experiences, preachers will almost surely be nourished by a new hearing of their own.

Although the "I" of the preacher appears in several of the following sermons, in no case is this "I" the primary focusing "eye" of the sermon. In *each* case, the preacher has attempted to stand and look and listen from within the world of distinctive listeners.

On the Sunday when **Margaret Schwarzer** preached her "Ruth and Naomi" sermon, normal church attendance was significantly increased by a sizable contingent of young women who had gathered at the church over the preceding weekend for an annual girls choir festival. The participants were accomplished and eager singers, yet many had no sense of support from, or personal place, in the church. They did not, as the preacher later observed, "sense The Story in *their* story." Thus, the preacher approached the biblical text with a desire "to make the ancient power of God's grace, and the abiding presence of God's love accessible" to these young women. The result is a sparkling retelling/rehearing of an old love story. The preacher gracefully uplifts the depths of God's covenant commitment to us, as is symbolized in the unlikely relationship, under tragic conditions, of a mother-in-law and her daughter-in-law.

A similar attentiveness to specific congregational concern is found in the sermon of Chaplain **James Adams**. It is delivered in a required chapel service for residential students of an Episcopal high school. Expecting to receive one more lecture on what religious regimens they are expected to shoulder in addition to their academic requirements and dormitory rules, the students experience an engaging surprise: much more freedom (and rather more responsibility) than many of them are probably quite ready to cope with. Without talking down to these adolescents, Adams levels with them at a point of predictable need, and does so with imagination and subtle empathy.

The congregation **Nathaniel Pierce** addresses is very different, requiring what he regards as "one of the toughest sermons I have ever written." A former pastor in a parish where, during his tenure, there were serious rector-vestry disagreements over Christian social vision, Pierce has been invited by the current rector to preach at Evensong during the celebration of the parish's one hundredth anniversary. The tasks of the sermon, as Pierce envisions them, are to bless and support his successor, to celebrate the accomplishments that the community shared while he was among them, to assure friends and supporters of his own continued well-being and commitment to social ministry— and to gently, firmly, clearly challenge the parish as well.

The audience for **Bishop Browning's** sermon also comes to church with ears particularly tuned. These are seminarians approaching ordination, listening to their chief pastor, who is himself coming to the conclusion of his responsibilities as Presiding Bishop in the Episcopal Church. The text, the appointed Evensong course reading from Paul's Epistle to the Galatians, provides an excellent context for addressing questions of ministerial authority and discernment.

In **Debra Metzgar's** sermon, the specific role of the congregation in the preacher's own hearing of the gospel is most explicit. Metzgar is also addressing the seminarian preaching conference. Yet it is two voices from two other congregations that give direction to this sermon: "A man I hardly knew and a three week old infant—these two became my teachers recently," she begins. Before the sermon is through, these teachers have become the new congregation's teachers also.

In each of these sermons, the voice of God's Spirit is heard as the conversations implicit in Scripture interact, through the homiletical artistry of the preacher, with the contemporary cries of God's people.

Entreat Me Not to Leave You:
A Feminine Icon of God's Covenant Love

A Sermon Preached by
The Reverend Margaret Schwarzer
October 15, 1995

Ruth 1: (1-7) 8-19a
Psalm 113
Luke 17: 11-19

∞

Our Western tradition offers us many cultural icons of male camaraderie; they range from the absurd to the profound: Butch Cassidy
had the Sundance Kid, the Lone Ranger had Tonto, Sherlock Holmes
had Watson, Othello had Iago, and even Don Quixote found a com-
rade in Sancho Panza. Obviously, some of these relationships are
more complicated than others, a few provide jealousy or betrayal with
the fellowship they offer, but our cultural wisdom about men's
friendships runs deep. It runs all the way back to some of Scripture's
earliest models of fellowship: Jesus' eating with his twelve disciples;
Jesus' special rapport with Peter; King David's fellowship with
Jonathan. Our Western culture offers us fewer images for the camaraderie among women or the companionship between women. In
fact, I couldn't think of any classic images of women's companionship that had the depth or resonance of the male friendships I have
cited. So when we come upon examples of women's camaraderie,
these models of companionship need to be celebrated and savored.
They need to be held up and appreciated for all the beauty and the
wisdom they hold.

This morning's Old Testament lesson plunges us into such a relationship between women. It is a vibrant, intimate exchange between
Ruth, a widow, and her mother-in-law, Naomi. This exchange hints at
a relationship that is one of Scripture's great icons for women's
friendship and women's camaraderie. In fact, the Book of Ruth, a
short four chapters long, is a gem of a story. It's a story pieced together to reveal the ways in which God can transform tragedy, a story that
shows grace flowing into women's lives and grace being forged
through women's choices. It is a record of women's camaraderie that
has been passed down for hundreds of generations.

But before we unpack the passionate friendship that binds these two together, we need to acknowledge the deep tragedy that works at pulling them apart. In the verses we read today, Naomi is counseling her two daughters-in-law to leave her and return to their own parents. Both of Naomi's sons have died and left two new widows, Ruth and Orpah, with the older widow, Naomi. Naomi urges her daughters-in-law to leave her because there is nothing left for three women to rebuild or renew. In ancient Israel, three women cut off from their patriarchal clan are three women in isolation. These three are cut off from all cultural support, from the possibility of owning property, and from all social status. They will soon be bereft of all material goods, because they do not have enough food to survive, there are no men to plough, no seeds to plant. And tragedy cuts deeper still, for these three women are bereft of their futures. They are bereft of all their dreams of children and grandchildren and the kind of human immortality that comes through birth. Finally, these three are in mourning. Ruth and Orpah grieve their dead husbands; Naomi grieves over the death of her only two sons. There is enough tragedy to justify their turning on one another in rage or despair. "Nothing" is all that is left. Each has a barren womb, stands in a barren place, sees a barren future.

Into this "nothing" Naomi speaks. She makes a joke out of misfortune. She finds a way to laugh at barrenness. The humor is dry, but so is the place she is standing. She spins out a spoof of what would happen if her two daughters-in-law stayed with her. "Even if you stay," she jokes, "and I gave birth to two new sons immediately, they would only be babies when you were ready to remarry, and if you waited till *they* were ready for marriage, *you* would be *too old*." There is humor in the image of baby boys marrying mature women, or in mature men marrying old ladies, but the humor is bitter because it also states Naomi's reality. If they stay with Naomi, Ruth and Orpah are caught between a rock and a hard place: barrenness lies in all directions. Naomi's joke is at her own expense, and she uses it to convince the two younger women she loves to forsake her and build a new life for themselves. Orpah is convinced by Naomi's painful logic; she kisses Naomi good-bye and sets out to return to her kinfolk. But Ruth—even in the face of certain failure, Ruth stands by Naomi.

If we know anything about the Book of Ruth, we know the next words Ruth speaks to Naomi, words of kinship so powerful they are often read at weddings, describing the romantic love between men and women. But these words begin as words that cemented a deep friendship between a widow and her mother-in-law:

> *"Entreat me not to leave you or return from following you;*
> *for where you go I will go, and where you lodge I will lodge;*
> *your people shall be my people, and your God my God;*
> *where you die I will die, and there will I be buried.*
> *May the Lord do so to me and more also*
> *if even death parts me from you."*

These are wonderful words to hear on the day when Neil, Tory, and Matthew have been baptized, for each parent, grandparent, and godparent lives out these words when they make a commitment to raise their child as a Christian. In these baptisms, the youngest members of three families have been told that they will never be forsaken; that our God is now their God, that even death will not part us from them. Today we welcome them, and they take their places as the newest members of a holy fellowship which spans 2,000 years of history.

"Entreat me not to leave you or return from following you . . ." All that can be pledged, Ruth pledges. She swears to follow her mother-in-law to the ends of the earth; she promises to live where she lives; accept as her kin any kin of Naomi's; accept as her God the God of Abraham Naomi worships. Ruth swears to be buried where Naomi is buried, even swears that the love between them is so strong that death will not separate them. In the midst of aridity, emptiness, and failure, Ruth gives to Naomi all she has to offer. Ruth offers her own life as a counterweight to the tragedies of Naomi's life. Ruth promises to endure, together, whatever life brings Naomi. Ruth commits her physical labor to improving Naomi's lot. It is only Ruth's promise that ensures that Naomi will not be stripped of her last human companion. To ensure that Naomi will not struggle alone, Ruth gives up her chance for a better life in her Moabite clan. Why does Ruth do this? The starkness of the story's beginning, which contains only barrenness for the three women, pushes us to understand that Ruth makes this pledge selflessly, against the equally selfless command of Naomi, who instructs Ruth to leave. Ruth does not love Naomi for what Naomi can give her. Naomi has nothing to give her. Ruth does not love Naomi because Ruth has no other options; Ruth would have a better chance for survival alone, without Naomi. Ruth loves Naomi because . . . Ruth loves *Naomi*. Because of the gifts and commitments knit into their past relationship Ruth will not put to one side the love she holds for Naomi. Ruth asserts that her primary identity rests in her relationship with her mother-in-law. Ruth answers Naomi's tragedy with integrity and faithfulness.

As the story continues, great things come from Ruth's passionate commitment to Naomi. Moving beyond the verses we heard today, the grace of Ruth's faithfulness transforms the barrenness of both women. When they reach Bethlehem, Ruth and Naomi are comrades, committed to each other's well-being. First they figure out a way for Ruth to get food. She walks behind the men who harvest the wheat and picks up the bits of wheat they leave behind, enough for a daily feast for two hungry women. As the wheat is gathered, Ruth meets the owner of the field, an unmarried man named Boaz. Together Ruth and Naomi devise a scheme so that the unmarried man will marry Ruth. The plan takes imagination and boldness, but Naomi and Ruth orchestrate it well. Out of their caring and love for each other, these two women conceive a life of hope and vitality in Bethlehem. Out of the fruitfulness of Ruth and Naomi's love comes a future neither one could have envisioned. Boaz turns out to be a relative of Naomi's, and he falls in love with Ruth and marries her. So Ruth and Boaz have a son. As the story ends, this new baby nestles in Naomi's arms as the women of Bethlehem tell Naomi "that this little boy will be to you a restorer of life and a nourisher of your old age, for your daughter-in-law who loves you, who is more to you than seven sons, has borne him." The love between these two women conceives a richer life for each one.

According to Jewish tradition, God loved the love between Ruth and Naomi; God loved the miracle of what they made between them through their faith and steadfastness. God so loved Ruth and Naomi that God chose the fruit of that love—the baby Obed—to be a member of the House of David. Obed became the grandfather of the great King David. And so the selfless love between these two women is also added to another son of the House of David, the son we name as Messiah. Christ comes from the House of David, and the lineage of Ruth. Out of a woman who offered her life as a counterweight to Naomi's tragedy, comes the Christ Child, who will offer his life as a counterweight for the sins of the whole world.

Like Christ's love, Ruth and Naomi's love is not meant to remain as a distant ideal, and it has not. In fact, when this story was first incorporated into the Jewish canon, the Book of Ruth had a measurable impact on the Jewish community. When they heard the story, the ruling elite were so struck by Naomi's destitution that they changed the laws of property and inheritance to allow widows to be property owners in certain circumstances. Though it did not take most widows out of poverty, this shift was a remarkable first step in a path toward economic justice for women. Ruth and Naomi's love healed each of them, became a foundation for the House of David, and is directly responsible for improving the lives of many widows whose names we will never know.

Ruth and Naomi are women whose courage and strength changed the course of history, but we are cheating Ruth and Naomi out of their proper places if we see them only as historical figures. The next time we see pictures of third-world women gathering wheat or rice, women of India, Asia, or Africa, we need to remember that Ruth and Naomi, too, gathered wheat and respect our modern sister's dignity and labor. Similarly, when we think of Ruth and Naomi's friendship, we need to remember that strong relationships are still being forged among women. Just as the laying on of hands has been passed on from generation to generation in the rites of Confirmation and Ordination, we can trust that Ruth and Naomi's friendship has been passed down from woman to woman and is still a part of our community. In the face of popular culture's tendency to hold up women's relationships as chatty and shallow, we will know better.

This story about a widow and her mother-in-law is not a small story. It ripples out into the history of the Jewish people. It ripples out into the history of Christian people. It offers us a different example of how to love as Christ loves us; it asks us to learn to love with the faithfulness of Ruth and with the steadfastness of Naomi.

Amen.

A Boat Like That Will Never Sink

Text of Sermon Preached by James P. Adams
Episcopal High School
Alexandria, Virginia

∞

Beginning in Northern New Hampshire, the Connecticut River flows south along the border between New Hampshire and Vermont and winds its way through Massachusetts and Connecticut until, some 407 miles later, it reaches salt water, where it whirls into Long Island Sound. At about mile 406 of those 407 winding river miles, just before the river makes its last big turn for home, lived an old owl of a man named Earl Brockway.

Earl Brockway spent his whole life building wooden workboats on his property in a Connecticut town called Old Saybrook. Earl's boat, known as the Brockway Scow, became rather famous in much of coastal New England for its rugged, seaworthy character. Earl built every scow with his own leathery hands—shaping and cutting every piece of wood, sealing and securing every seam, pounding every nail. Even when business flourished, Earl worked alone. My grandfather says that the Coast Guard had never been called to rescue anyone in a Brockway Scow. If you were lucky enough to own a Brockway Scow, you owned a twenty-foot-long workboat with a flat bottom and a square hull that would never, ever sink.

When my father turned forty, he gave Earl Brockway $2,500 and fulfilled a lifelong desire. He got himself a Brockway Scow. For another $500, Earl would have sanded, sealed, and painted it pea green, but my father was (and still is) a thrifty Yankee. So at thirteen years of age, I was given my first chance at a true religious work. I would spend that summer on the banks of the Connecticut River—at Earl Brockway's outdoor workshop—sanding, sealing, and painting my father's Brockway Scow.

Working there, surrounded by embryonic workboats, I witnessed a steady flow of pilgrims who came to meet Earl and see him at his craft. He never stopped working. People came to see the long lengths of lumber crossed over fifty-gallon oil drums bending naturally, over several weeks time, to the shape that Earl needed. Like inquisitive disciples, before they left, they'd all ask Earl the same question: "What's your secret? What makes your boat so seaworthy?"

Earl worked as they talked, and he answered the same way each time, always as though it were the first time he'd heard the question. "The Brockway Scow," he would say, "the Brockway Scow is a boat that knows its true center. The ocean can't hurt a boat that knows its true center. A boat like that will never sink."

I've got to believe that Jesus has a special love for Earl Brockway. Today, Jesus calls upon us to define our center. "No slave can serve two masters, for a slave will either hate the one and love the other, or be devoted to the one and despise the other. You cannot serve God and wealth." Jesus is saying, "You can serve only one master; who or what will it be?" It sounds as though you and I have a choice.

What a mysterious blessing! The Lord of the universe is saying to us, "What gets you out of bed in the morning? What are you all about? What floats your boat? Upon what or whom are you building your life? What is the center of your world?"

Responding to a recent survey, incoming freshmen at Harvard University listed as their top three life goals: money, power, and prestige. Interesting. Maybe there will be a point in your life, maybe now, when your top three goals will be money, power, and prestige. Your life is a gift from God. What you make of it can be your gift back to God, or it can be something else.

The philosopher Kierkegaard said, "Life can only be understood backwards, but it must be lived forwards." So what does life look like in the rearview mirror? Suppose you knew that you were dying. The doctors say that your condition is terminal. What would your top life goals be then? Do you think that money, power, and prestige would even make the list?

As a part-time hospital chaplain, I've had the opportunity to spend time with a number of people in the last days or hours of their lives. The oldest and perhaps the most memorable was Margaret Fenton. She was ninety-eight years old when she contracted pneumonia. She was unable to fight it effectively and landed in the intensive care unit at Georgetown University Hospital. I saw Mrs. Fenton every day and every visit began the same way. This lovely old woman thought of life as important business. So every visit she would place her century-old hands in mine and say. "Chaplain, how's business?" I never knew how to answer that question. But it didn't matter. She wanted to pray together and we did—every day. She was well aware that she was dying, and we faced the end with steadfast faith, honest about her fears, and sure about her life goals.

One day I asked her, "Mrs. Fenton, have you always been such a spiritual person?"

Her answer blew me away. "No, can't say that I have. I spent the first half of my life trying to do it my way, self-centered, without God. By the time I was forty-five, I was miserable. So I went down to the church and turned myself in!" Margaret Fenton died two days later, in the hope of heaven. I have no doubt that she's looking down on us tonight and asking, "How's business?"

I've got news for you. The human condition is terminal. Life is precious and short. *Jesus loves you.* He loves you more than you know. *He's crazy about you.* So what are you supposed to do? He wants you to follow your heart's deepest desires: be a banker or a boat builder. Be a teacher or a train conductor. Be a football player or a pharmacist. Be a doctor or a dancer. Be a dad or a mom. Be a lawyer or a librarian. Be a headmaster or a homemaker. Be a piano player or a preacher. Be a senator or a singer. Who knows, you might even become rich and powerful. Whatever career path you follow, life will sometimes be like a dream come true, and sometimes life is a living nightmare. Through it all, the hands of God in Jesus Christ will be reaching out to you. Those hands are as strong and steady as Earl Brockway's boat-building hands and as loving and gentle as Margaret Fenton's praying hands. You can build your life around them. All that you have to do, when you're ready, is reach out and take his hand. It's an open lifelong invitation. You can accept it when you're eight or ninety-eight. You can make your life a gift to God. But at your core, at your very center, you must decide what gives your life meaning and direction. You must decide what will sustain you through the storms of life. *You must decide what you believe.*

This summer, I visited my parents at their home in Connecticut. On the second morning of my visit I was awakened by the unpleasant sounds of someone using power tools. These were loud power tools, and it was around seven in the morning. I pulled myself out of bed and looked out the bedroom window. There, out at the edge of the yard, I saw my teenage brother running a power sander. In front of him, straddled on two fifty-gallon oil drums was the old Brockway Scow, now seventeen years old. The scow had been retired to the backyard for almost ten years. I heard my father in the kitchen. I called to him, "Dad, what's Seth doing out there?"

"Oh, he's trying to resurrect the old Brockway. I hope it floats!" he laughed.

I answered him quickly, "A Brockway Scow knows its true center. A boat like that will never sink."

Is the Meter Sitting on the Floor?

A sermon by the Rev. Nathaniel W. Pierce
at All Saints Parish, Brookline, Massachusetts

(The Rev. Nathaniel W. Pierce is presently the Rector of Great Choptank Parish, Christ Episcopal Church, in Cambridge, Maryland.)

∞

I want to express my gratitude to your Rector, the Rev. David Killian, for inviting me to preach here today. As this parish celebrates 100 years of mission and ministry in Brookline and to the wider church, it is a time to celebrate and to remember.

When Audrey and I moved into the rectory next door to this church in the fall of 1984, the renovation work was coming to an end. Thus, we were quite used to various odds and ends being taken care of as we settled into our new home. As the electricians completed their part, I asked about the electric meter that was sitting on the floor of the furnace room. "Only Boston Edison can install that," I was told, "and they should be around in the next couple of weeks." Meanwhile the gap in the line left by the missing meter had been bridged and we had electricity throughout the house.

I think it was in December that I suddenly realized that Boston Edison did not have 1789 Beacon Street on its list of homes requiring a visit. When I called the company about this, I was told that the town of Brookline needed to approve the work that had been done, particularly from a safety standpoint, before the meter could be reinstalled. When I called the town inspector, he told me that the town had already signed off on the project and sent the necessary forms to Boston Edison.

The Meter on the Floor

Meanwhile, I took a special interest in Stanley, the older gentleman who came faithfully to our door every month to read the electric meter. I accompanied him down the stairs to the basement and watched as he flashed his light on the meter that was lying on the floor, unconnected to anything. He dutifully entered the numbers in his hand-held electronic recorder. "I don't think the numbers have changed much since last month," I said to him. "Nope," he replied, "they probably haven't." And then he was off to his next call.

Well, the whole situation struck me as being utterly absurd. What a waste of time to have someone come to the house once a month to read a meter that did not change. I called Boston Edison again and was connected with a recently hired young MIT engineer. Since I am a graduate of the Cornell Engineering School, we chatted a bit about our respective educational experiences and then got down to brass tacks. She explained to me that she had designed and implemented a computer program that carefully monitored the electrical consumption at every meter read by Boston Edison. Significant changes received some follow-up attention. "So," said I, "if a meter suddenly went from 2,000 kilowatts a month to zero, your program would pick this up?" "But of course," came the exasperated reply. "That would be a very dramatic change indeed."

Next month Stanley came and read the meter which by now had not changed in six months. I asked him if there wasn't something he could do. He punched his little keyboard furiously and said, "There, that should get their attention." But it didn't. One last phone call to a Boston Edison vice president was equally unproductive. The meter remained on the floor, the church paid nothing for the electricity we were using in the rectory, and I seemed to be the only person concerned about it. What would you do? To whom do you turn?

Finally, I appealed to the court of last resort, the one place that had a strong record of sorting out such absurdities and that accepted inquiries from just about anyone. I wrote a letter to *Ask the Globe*. I explained the situation and my unsuccessful efforts over the past seven months to rectify it. *The Boston Globe* made some phone calls and then printed the story; success at last. Boston Edison got its act together; it was determined that the town inspector had not signed off on the installation after all. He somewhat sheepishly arrived a few days later and pronounced the work safe and up to code.

He was followed by a crew from Boston Edison, which dusted off the meter and installed it. I was pleased and Stanley was pleased.

I then called Boston Edison again to thank the company for its assistance in resolving the issue. I asked how it wanted to handle the eight months of free electricity we had received in the rectory, which is, after all, a seven-bedroom, six-fireplace house. Boston Edison in turn expressed regret that I had had so much difficulty with the situation myself and said that there would be no charge.

I tell you this true story not only because it seems to typify so many issues in our modern culture, but also because for me it is a parable about our church. We in the Episcopal Church do a very good job of "reading the meter." That is to say, we baptize, confirm, marry, and bury people in need of such services. We keep meticulous records on these sacraments as well as on attendance and carry out the liturgy of the church in a finer, more tasteful fashion than anyone else. But what is our meter plugged into? Is it plugged into anything at all, much less connected to God?

I have read with great interest about the "Ruah" program which has been initiated by David Killian here at All Saints. In the study of various other spiritual disciplines, we may indeed be empowered to discern the work of the Spirit more clearly in our own. But we need to recognize, particularly because we are Christians active in a church, that we may in fact be the very people who are deaf and blind to what God is calling us to do. We may have become Christians who dare not venture into the unknown.

A Venturesome Spirit

In its early days members of this parish did have some of this venturesome spirit. As you can see, they thought on a grand scale when this building was designed and built. More significantly, they gave a young, untested, unknown artist his very first commission as a creator of stained glass windows. So, the very first window by Charles J. Connick (and the first stained glass window here at All Saints) in the Langdon Chapel bears eloquent testimony to that venturesome spirit that was present here at All Saints in 1910.

Members of this parish were so pleased with this window that Connick was commissioned in 1912 to do a second one. Shortly thereafter he was able to open his studio in Boston on Harcourt Street, down near what is now known as Copley Place. From there he launched his crusade to rescue the art form from the dark ages of sentimental realism that had reigned throughout the nineteenth century.

As an aside and by way of contrast, Trinity Church in Copley Square, Boston, commissioned almost all of its windows from long-established studios in England during an era when anything from England was thought to be superior. In so doing, Trinity managed to overlook one of the greatest artists of all time located literally three blocks away from its front door. For when Charles J. Connick died in 1945, his *New York Times* obituary noted that he was "considered the world's greatest contemporary craftsman in stained glass."

Over the years many other Connick windows were commissioned by

All Saints Parish. However, by 1986 the average age of the Connick employees was 79 and the decision was made to close the studio. They accepted their last order, fittingly, for the Langdon Chapel here at All Saints. The window was funded by a bequest from Henry Pepper and appropriately portrays the history of this parish that Henry and his wife, Shirley, loved so dearly for so many years.

Fortunately, there is an award-winning documentary on the making of the Pepper window by the noted filmmaker, John Bishop. The film includes not only some rare footage of Connick himself, but also a portion of the dedicatory service here at All Saints. But the film's real accomplishment, I think, is that it manages to capture something of the spirit and sense of community that permeated the Connick Studio for seventy-four years.

This documentary, called *The Last Window,* premiered in this very building in December 1988. No doubt this moving, informative, extraordinary film has been shown here yet once again as part of your centennial celebration. Recall with me now those marvelous words of Charles Connick with which John Bishop ended his magnificent film (with apologies for the sexist language):

> *I want to make beautiful interiors for both churches and souls. I want men to hear my windows singing; to hear them singing of God; I want men to know that God is at the core of their own souls.*

Here was an artist truly connected to a spiritual realm beyond the ordinary, and here was a church that was able to recognize and honor that. As you celebrate your first 100 years, take some well-deserved pride in the role this parish played in launching the career of one of the great American artists of the twentieth century.

The Pepper window was a continuing thread of my ministry here at All Saints. I made one of my first pastoral calls on Henry and Shirley in their home in Wellesley. I officiated at Henry's funeral and then worked with the Connick Studio in designing the window itself. The dedicatory service in 1986 was well covered by local TV stations. For the next two years I helped John Bishop to secure the necessary funding for his wonderful documentary.

A History of Peacemaking

When I resigned as rector four months after the film's premiere, I was able to give more of my time to my other major project: a book on the history of the peace movement in the Episcopal Church, which was published in the fall of 1989.

When I told a friend about this book I was writing in collaboration with Dr. Paul Ward, he said: "A book on the history of the peace movement in the Episcopal Church; are all the pages blank?" For the years before 1917, the pages would indeed be blank. But something dramatic happened in 1917, which changed our church. This brings me to the remarkable story of Paul Jones, my third and last story for you this afternoon.

Jones, a graduate of the Episcopal Theological School here in Cambridge, was elected bishop of the Missionary District of Utah in 1914. In 1917 he uttered three words that threw the Episcopal Church into turmoil. These three words prompted two separate investigations of Jones by his fellow bishops and forced him to suspend his promising work as the bishop of Utah.

And what were these three words? What three words could bring down such anger and criticism on a bishop of our church in 1917? Jones had dared to say: "War is unchristian."

Of course, the war fever that was then sweeping the United States made such a statement controversial. But we today may not fully appreciate the feelings about the First World War that permeated the Anglican Communion of which the Episcopal Church is a part. Consider, for example, these words taken from a 1915 sermon preached by the bishop of London, the third-ranking prelate in the English Church: "Kill Germans: kill the good as well as the bad, kill the young men as well as the old, kill those who have shown kindness to our wounded. As I have said a thousand times, I look upon it as a war for purity."

Similar feelings were present in our own House of Bishops, and thus it should come as no surprise that the second Committee of Bishops investigating Jones concluded in more sedate language: "This [Episcopal] Church . . . is practically a unit in holding that [war] is not an unchristian thing. In the face of this unanimity, it is neither right or wise for a trusted bishop to declare and maintain that it is an unchristian thing. The Bishop of Utah ought to resign his office."

A graceful accommodation was reached, and on April 11, 1918, Paul Jones submitted his resignation as the Bishop of the Missionary District of Utah. In his almost Christlike farewell to his diocese, Jones said: "Where I serve the Church is of small importance so long as I can make my life count in the cause of Christ."

Yet the Episcopal Church was not quite finished with Jones. He had been invited to preach at the alumni service during commencement at the seminary that had prepared him for ministry. In the spring of 1918 he was asked to withdraw by representatives of the Episcopal Theological School "in order that a timely war sermon might be preached" by Bishop Lawrence of Massachusetts. Jones graciously complied; for as long as he lived, he never again attended a meeting of the House of Bishops, although that body did pass a resolution in 1934, sixteen years after his forced resignation, saying that they missed his presence at their meetings.

One can only wonder whether the passage from the prophet Jeremiah for today's service was all that familiar to our bishops of that era. Let us not forget that when Jeremiah speaks of "those whose ears are closed, who cannot listen to the Word of the Lord," these are words addressed not only to the people of the Covenant who lived 2,500 years ago, they are words that are addressed very specifically to each and every one of us in our own time.

A Ministry of Peace and Conscience

The Diocese of Maine took Bishop Jones in for a year after his resignation; he served two small missions there. Then he accepted a position with the Fellowship of Reconciliation, which allowed him to travel the country speaking about the importance of conscience in matters of religious faith. In his later years he was Chaplain at Antioch College in Ohio. In 1939, two years before his death, Jones agreed to be one of the founding members of the Episcopal Pacifist Fellowship, now known as the Episcopal Peace Fellowship, or EPF.

Thus, in the fall of 1989, when the final draft of the history was presented to the board of the EPF, Paul Ward and I put forward a recommendation: that the EPF undertake the challenging task of persuading the Standing Liturgical Commission and the General Convention of the Episcopal Church to add Paul Jones to our Calendar of Saints. The leadership of the EPF agreed, and thus began what has turned out to be an eight-year effort.

The Diocese of Arizona was the first to call for Jones to be added to our Calendar; other dioceses, including this one, followed with similar resolutions. My own Diocese of Easton was one of the last.

The proposal to add Jones to the Calendar of Saints was being put forward to an Episcopal Church that was vastly different from the one of 1918. Our church had recognized the validity of the position of a conscientious objector to war in 1934. By 1962 our House of Bishops was calling for a major church program on the work for peace.

A National Peace Commission

Perhaps, however, the most significant action initiated by our church on peace-related issues came in 1985 when the General Convention created the Standing Commission on Peace, a permanent body that would now report directly to the Convention at each triennial meeting. Thus, the Peace Commission joined Liturgy, Music, Mission, Ecumenical Affairs, and other commissions at the very center of our church's decision-making process.

It was my privilege to serve as the first chair of the Standing Commission on Peace from 1986 to 1988. The Rev. Jane Garrett of the Diocese of Vermont served as chair from 1989 to 1991, and in a delightful, ironic twist of history, the third chair was none other than the present dean of the very seminary that would not permit Jones to speak, that wanted to hear a war sermon and not a peace sermon in 1918, the Very Rev. William Rankin.

And so it came to pass that in the summer of 1994 the first step to add Bishop Paul Jones to our Calendar of Saints was taken by our General Convention. The proposal will be tested for three years, and final action should come in 1997.

The story of Paul Jones will now be told each and every year, with its important lesson that those who are absolutely sure of God's will, even if they be the entire House of Episcopal Bishops, may in fact be quite wrong. As Cardinal Cushing of Boston once said: "Saints are okay in Heaven, but they're Hell on earth."

And so I have shared with you this afternoon three quite different stories: one of a man who read an electric meter unconnected to anything for eight months, one of a church willing to give an untested artist in stained glass his very first commission, and one of a bishop who dared to say, "War is unchristian." Which story is your story?

Has your understanding of God changed in the last five or ten years? Faithful as you may be in your Christian duty, are you really connected to God? Or is the spiritual meter you are reading in reality sitting on the floor, unconnected to anything? Where do you feel that you are taking a risk in your own spiritual journey? These are some of the questions which these stories put before all of us this afternoon.

I close with a collect for the day, September 4, on which Paul Jones will now be remembered in our beloved church. Let us pray.

> *Loving God, Creator and Sustainer of humanity, to whom each person is sacred and for whom all wars are unchristian: Raise up in*

*this and every land and time courageous women and men who, like
your servant Paul Jones, will stand firm in proclaiming the gospel
of peace when the multitude is clamoring for war, and who will
dare to call your church to fulfill her reconciling vocation. This we
ask in the name of the One who calls us to peace and reconciliation,
your Son our Savior Jesus Christ; who lives and reigns with you and
the Holy Spirit, one God, now and for ever. Amen.*

The Communal Dimensions of Vocational Discernment

The Most Rev. Edmond L. Browning
Presiding Bishop of the Episcopal Church

∞

But when God, who set me apart from birth and called me by his grace,
was pleased to reveal his son in me so that I might preach him among the
gentiles, I did not consult any man, nor did I go up to Jerusalem to see
those who were apostles before I was . . .

Galatians 1: 15-17

I'm sure that St. Paul's brief account of his own discernment process
strikes a responsive chord in some of you: apparently, he began what
we would all have to say was a very successful ministry without a
weekend with his commission on ministry, with no appearance before
the standing committee, without writing even one ember day letter,
without having taken the General Ordination Exams. How on earth
did he manage? Those were the days. Also called to preach the gospel,
your experience is very different.

We have trained ourselves to be suspicious of people like Paul. We
refer to them as "lone wolves," and we are apt to regard them as dangerous.

If your discernment process included a period of time in which
your call had not yet been recognized in an official way—if you were
in seminary for a while before becoming a postulant, for instance—
you know firsthand that the church is uncertain just how to
approach people who assert a call before that recognition happens,
and you know that this uncertainty is painful for the one who asserts
the call.

We now bring layer upon layer of discernment to bear on an individual's assertion of calling—something the folks in Jerusalem apparently wanted to do with Paul, and eventually did do. After a few years,
they all sat down together to see if they were all preaching the same
thing, if all could be agreed that Paul represented the faith appropriately when he spoke in Jesus' name. We know that Paul did not enjoy
himself very much at what we have come to call the Council of
Jerusalem. He hated having his authority questioned and was never
shy about asserting it. We recognize our own impatient spirits in his,
our own impatience with having to tell yet another committee yet

another time all about how we first discerned God's call to us.

It is hard for us to answer skepticism about what, to us, is very clear: "God has called me to proclaim the good news of Christ to the world. This is what I was born to do." It is so clear to us; we are shaken when it is not immediately self-evident to everyone else.

Where *does* our authority to preach come from? You may indeed survive thirty committees and a psychiatrist, but you know that your authority does not come from them. All they are doing is trying their best to hear in you the call you have already heard. They don't create the call in you. The call comes from God. They are there doing their best to represent the community God called you to serve. They are exercising *their* call to discernment.

The time in your life when you are preparing for the ordained ministry, of which preaching is so vital a part, is a good time to learn these frustrating lessons about how the community's discernment of gifts for ministry is related to God's call to ministry. For this will not be the last time you will be called upon to claim and justify your call: the response of the people you seek to serve to your self-presentation will form your ministry for as long as it lasts. Nobody ministers alone—we do it in the midst of the Body of Christ, in partnership with the brothers and sisters among whom God has placed us. The gifts we have been given, although they have been given to us, are really not *for* us—they are for them.

God builds the Body through us; that's what the gifts of ministry are for. However magnificent a voice or penetrating an intellect a preacher may possess, there is one and only one criterion for his or her success in preaching the word: that the people are edified. If the people are built and strengthened by your ministry, it is in line with God's purpose. If they are not, no matter how brilliant to you it may be, it has fallen short of what God intended for it.

How will you know? Don't worry—they will tell you. People are only too glad to let you know exactly where it is that you have fallen short.

Our line of work is not for the thin-skinned. We learn very quickly, if we continue in ordained ministry, to handle negative criticism that can be very personal at times. Imagine, for a moment, knowing what you know about this church at this time in history, the mail that comes across my desk. You can imagine that it's not all love letters.

But it will be the same for you; people bring all manner of needs to the priest, and sometimes they are quick to condemn us for not being able to meet those needs. Here the discernment needed is yours, and that of your brother and sister clergy: to which criticisms should you respond with changed behavior, and which arise from causes much too large and deep for you to remedy, causes that really don't have much to do with you at all? We are called by God, but we are not called to *be* God. Over and over, people will hope that you can somehow become God for them, and you cannot. Be faithful and passionate in prayer about these people. Lean on the counsel of those who have worked in this vineyard for a long time, on those brothers and sisters whom you know and whose wisdom you trust, who love you and the church enough to tell you the truth. Don't discern your response to your peoples' response all by yourself. Do what even cranky St. Paul ended up doing, probably against his will: get help in discernment from the others who are also called to this ministry. Maybe he didn't want to examine his call with Peter and James and John. Maybe it went against the grain of his pride. But eventually he had to. He was called by God, but he lived in the church. Eventually, the church had to call him. We don't know another way to discern the call of God besides the one they used: to sit down together and get a sense of how it is that the gospel will be proclaimed by this person in this church at this time.

I believe with all my heart that the person called by God and raised up by the church to preach in the name of Christ cannot fail in this sacred ministry *if* he or she is open to the guidance of the Holy Spirit. That doesn't mean, of course, that all such people will be successful in the world's eyes. Paul and all of the apostles who discerned his ministry were killed, for heaven's sake. That's not what the world thinks of as a howling success.

We do not speak of success in terms of prosperity, but rather in terms of building up the Body of Christ. That is why we can venerate the martyrs of our faith: death is the ultimate failure of human strength, but the church is stronger for their deaths. The ordinary, day-to-day suffering of all people derives new meaning from their example and witness; we join them in their deaths as well as in their lives, just as we do not behold Jesus' life apart from his death and resurrection. Successful? If we are faithful to God's call, we cannot be otherwise. However long or short our ministries, however powerful a position we may occupy in the church one day—these things almost don't matter. Only one thing matters. To hear the call and respond faithfully. All the rest will be revealed.

To bring your faithfulness to the sermon requires that you bring yourself. There is nothing that happens in the life of a priest that cannot be used to edify others. But there is nothing less edifying than the personal anecdotes of a preacher who believes himself to be exemplary. It is not in our moral triumphs and spiritual strengths that we lead the people of God best; it is in our weakness. People will learn far more from your story of God's transforming an error of yours into a moment of grace than they ever would learn from your description of your own virtuous handling of a situation. A sermon may be full of me and my family, but if it is not really about God's action instead of my own, I'm better off keeping it to myself.

I may—and I do—use all manner of material from my own life, but I must never use a word of it unless it shows the hand of God very clearly. To do otherwise would be to subject my hearers to a commercial about myself, and that would be pretty grim. Do you remember Paul's description of being swept up to heaven in a mystical vision? Remember how coy he was in his language when he talked about it: "I know a man . . ." he begins, unwilling to come right out and say that it was he himself of whom he spoke. He knew the power of preaching and the danger of it for the preacher, how a preacher's experience can attract or repel the hearer, depending on how it is used. Words have great power. We cannot use them lightly.

"Build the body," the Spirit commanded Paul, and he lived and worked in awe of that command. We must do the same. Does it build the Body? Will they grow and strengthen because of what I say? For this I am here, for this I was called. If the awesome power of this call is uppermost in my heart and mind, God will not fail to use me to gather and strengthen God's people. After all, does God bring us together so that we will not grow? So that we will become weaker? Does God assemble us in order that we may not deepen in faith and corporate love? I don't think so.

Thinking about preaching before I did it was a scary thing. I remember how scary it seemed, even though that was years and years ago. I think it's scary for most people. The remarkable thing is that it is still scary to me, in a way, even though I've done so much of it after all these years. I think other preachers feel the same, most of them.

We are still in awe of it. And we are right to be in awe of it—the touch of God on the preacher is powerful. We are not the same once we have been used by God in that way.

I wish you success in your preaching, then, not success as the world measures success, but a higher success. I wish you the knowledge that you have preached faithfully from a position of authentic trust in God's love for the people committed to your charge. I wish you the self-transcendence that can use even your weakness to strengthen others. I wish you the awe of preaching, the fear of it; may it never lose its scariness. And I wish you the courage of it, courage born of trust in the God who does not desert us. There is no greater joy than the knowledge that one is being used by God. May your joy be as full as mine has been these forty plus years, and may God bless you all. Amen.

Proclaiming Our Peculiarity

Sermon preached by the Rev. Debra Metzgar
Assist. Rector, Holy Innocents Church, Atlanta, Georgia

1 Peter 1: 3-5, 2: 9-10, John 9: 1, 5-12

∞

A man I hardly knew and a three-week-old infant—these two became my teachers recently. They gave me a fresh glimpse of what it means to proclaim Christ in a world so short on community and so long on divisiveness. I encountered my first gospel-bearer on a visit to the small congregation where I used to worship on a regular basis. It lies in a poverty-stricken and largely unnoticed urban neighborhood, and it's attended by people who, just like their neighborhood, are largely unseen by the world around them. Many of the regular worshipers live in group homes for the mentally ill, and, among other things, this means that the preacher/celebrant learns quickly to expect the unexpected during any given liturgy. The phrase "the prayers of the people" takes on a whole new meaning with this crowd! It is *not* the place for people who like their liturgies neat and tidy and "just the way we've always done it."

The man who gave me fresh vision is a person the world around him rarely sees. It is hard to exaggerate the myriad ways our larger culture discounts him. In a society that values monetary wealth, he stands as someone who has never heard of stock options and who likely has no checking account. In a world where white skin is still claimed by many to hold more value, he stands as one with dark brown coloring. In a world that says being articulate and silver tongued is a requirement of success, for preachers or anyone else, he stands by with a hopelessly garbled speech impediment that can try the patience even of those straining hard to decipher the message. His speech is slow and labored and *loud*—and in a room full of worshipers trying, more or less, to stay on the same page, his voice tags along half a phrase back, finishing every sentence long after the rest of the little crew has moved on to something else. He gets left behind in this world in more ways than one.

This Easter, the community held its first Easter Vigil. I have a hunch that this particular crowd understood those symbols of longing and light and dark, of identity and liberation, better than most. I know at least one person did: my new acquaintance, he of the garbled speech, was baptized that night, going down into the darkness of death and rising again to the light and life of Christ. He stood proudly at the font, the vicar told me, and when he was marked with the sign of Christ, he looked the priest straight in the eye and said, "Now I belong."

"Now I belong," he said. "Once you were not a people, but now you are God's people. Once you had not obtained mercy, but now you have obtained mercy. You are a chosen race, a chosen *ethnos*, a royal priesthood, a holy nation. You are a people of God's own choosing, God's own possession. Now you belong."

Fifty days later, on the Feast of Pentecost, a second baptism took place back in my hometown. On some counts, it could hardly have been more different. My godson was three weeks old, so this time the candidate was sleeping soundly in his mother's arms. His garb consisted not of Salvation Army cast-offs, but of the full white drape of the family christening gown. (His father swore it was the last time his son would wear a dress, but I reminded him that if he grew up to be ordained, he'd get to wear a dress every Sunday!)

This baptism was in a different city, in a very different parish, and occurred in the midst of what, in the world's eyes, was a very different crowd. We were what society calls "sound of mind." Most of us were Caucasian, and all of us knew what stock options were. Between the child's parents and godparents there were nine graduate degrees represented around the font. We were a crowd, in short, that the world looks at and declares, "You belong."

When we got to the renunciations, those of us speaking on David's behalf stood and faced the west doors that open out onto the world— a world that saw our Pentecost crowd as more valuable than the little Vigil crowd, a world that said race and class and education and social standing were significant determinants of a human being's worth, that define who "belongs" and who doesn't. We faced that world and its "take" on the universe and said that we renounced it, and that we turned around, quite literally in our pew, and accepted Jesus as our Savior, that we agreed to see life not with the world's eyes, but with Christ's eyes. We were saying to David that he belonged, that he was part of a matrix that has God as its reference point, that he was connected to this larger family before he ever knew any other way of seeing himself situated in the world, that he was not simply a *person* of God, but part of the *people* of God.

David, of course, was oblivious to all of this, understood none of it.

It would dawn on him only gradually. But I suddenly realized that the rest of us gathered there were not so different from our newest brother in Christ. Like David, we understood only partially the full reality of our identities in Christ and their implications for us and for our world.

We are reminded in this morning's lessons that the One who is the Light of the World comes to heal our sight, to let us see ourselves and those around us with the clarity of gospel vision. And we forget sometimes just how strange that gospel vision is.

It's a reminder that Peter hands us in his epistle. The phrase in that letter rendered "a people of God's own choosing," which says so much to us about gospel identity and belonging, has seen a variety of English translations. My personal favorite is the seventeenth-century King James Version. "You are," it says, "a peculiar people." On the days when I am exasperated with the church and fed up with the things we fight over, it seems a particularly apt phrase. We are, indeed, a peculiar people.

But there are other times, times connected to our truest selves and our deepest gospel callings, when we are strange and peculiar for *different* reasons. On those days it's our vision that is odd, and not our squabbling. On those days we see ourselves and our world in new and peculiar ways. We see that we *do* belong, but not for all the reasons that the world outside those west doors would claim. We catch a vision of a world in which baby David and my new acquaintance with the garbled speech would be seen not as members of two *different* races, but as members of a *chosen* race, the chosen *ethnos* of God. We begin to see that the lines we draw around one another don't show up in the same places as the *deeper* lines, drawn by a Divine Hand, that draw us in and bind us together.

The list of lines that you and I draw is bounded only by the human capacity to divide and separate: we draw them around nationality or class or skin color or the gender of the person we find ourselves loving. My own, well-worn list can include lines drawn around who you voted for in the last election, or whether your christology is like mine, or whether you like to do evangelism the way I do it.

The story of the man born blind reminds us this morning that the question of who belongs—that deepest longing of all of our hearts—is a question not answered in the ways that we, or the world, are tempted to answer it. The gospel vision is much more peculiar than that. The Fourth Evangelist makes it clear that the lines are drawn, not where we so often place them, but simply around whether, and how, a person sees Jesus. The man born blind, the "outsider," came to see Jesus clearly—and the religious leaders, the "church folk" of the day, did not. It was as simple as that.

The great good news to all of us is that we already belong, that we are already God's own possession. But possessed people act in strange and peculiar ways. They don't see the world the way everyone else sees it. And here's another catch: possessed people are precisely that—*possessed*. They belong to someone else. Their lives are not their own. The good news for us is: We already belong. *God* has a claim on our lives. And the gospel challenge to us is: We already belong. God has a *claim* on our lives. The blind man in John finds healing when he washes in a pool called "Sent." And the chosenness and belonging spoken of by Peter are set in the context of a contingent phrase: "You are a chosen people, God's own possession, *in order that* you may *proclaim* the mighty acts of the One who called you out of darkness and into his marvelous light." Healing belongs with being "sent," with mission, and identity—belonging—comes with a call to proclamation.

So listen up, preachers! Listen up, you who are called to proclaim! Know that you are loved by God, that you are held deep in the heart of the One who created you. Know, like my friend at the Vigil did, that you already belong. Recognize yourself as part of a people, a people with boundaries sketched not by human sinfulness, but by the boundless grace of God. Embrace the vocation that is given to all the holy people of God. Be possessed. Be peculiar. And don't be afraid to proclaim it.

Section III

"They Gave the Sense, So That the People Understood the Reading"
The Voice of the Spirit in the Pulses of Liturgy

THE VOICES OF SCRIPTURE, PREACHERS, AND CONGREGATIONS regularly convene for sacred conversation, but that regularity is often punctuated by special occasions. Such occasions can make rich contributions if they are allowed to have their own distinctive "say." In the overall adventure of life in the Spirit, probably no particular day is ultimately more important than any other. Yet some of the days of our lives are significant in ways that are clearly out of the ordinary.

High times of community celebration—be they times marked by special joy, fresh grief, or by holiday observances on designated dates—all of these invite attention to what might be called the "liturgical voices" that are essential dialogue partners in the sacred conversation of preaching. Consciously or unconsciously on such occasions, those who come to church are clearly asking, "Is there a Word from the Lord for us on a day like *this*?"

In the following section you will encounter sermons, each of which could be appropriately preached only on the particular day on which it was presented, and which very much *needed* to be preached.

The first of these days into which you are invited to enter imaginatively is the occasion of a requiem for a young woman. After years of mental illness, Ann Bjorkman Taylor took her own life, despite competent and compassionate efforts by her Christian family, friends, and professional counselors to support her and to help her toward healing. In addition to the predictable dynamic of grief that attends any death, the preacher, **Dayle Casey**, is faced with the crushing and disorienting psychological forces that accompany a suicide, as well as questions arising from the unforgiving moral attitude toward the taking of one's own life that has persisted in the history of the church. This tragic situation provides the preacher a challenging opportunity to present familiar Scriptures in fresh and hopeful ways.

The second day's observance to which you are invited is the celebration of Christmas Eve, with its predictable influx of "Christmas-and-Easter-only" worshipers. The invitation to a celebration of God's incarnation, in this particular case, is focused in dialogue with the "voice" of an explicitly congregational concern: the vicar, **Beth Wickenberg Ely**, will soon be leaving the parish with whom she is preaching on this holy night, for another pastoral assignment. The date of her departure, in fact, is imminent—only a week away. The invitation to "Carry the Child," therefore, comes with an additional level of meaning on this Christmas Eve for this parish.

The third day of significance is the day of an ordination to the priesthood. The preacher, **Meredith Potter**, knows each of the ordinands personally. With an unusual approach to the appointed lessons that is drawn from her experience, she gently, deftly puts the ordinands "in their place."

What does one say on All Saint's Day in the local parish, or on Trinity Sunday to a temporarily convened community of seminarian preachers? Listen to **William Eakins** and **Mitties De Champlain** as they orchestrate the distinctive liturgical voices with the voices of the Scriptures and the voices of their respective congregations.

The work of all these preachers stands in the tradition of the prophet Ezra. At the Festival of Booths in September 458 B.C.E., Ezra gathered the children of Israel who had returned from exile. Ezra was determined to reconstruct a social order consonant with God's Covenant. The Festival of Booths was a high holy day, deeply embedded in the tradition and the liturgical life of the Hebrew community. On this particular occasion, it pulsed with many layers of meaning. It pulsed as well with the people's profoundly conflicting feelings of gratitude and guilt, joy and relief, hope and fear.

Ezra convened the entire community—men and women "all who could hear with understanding." It was, understandably, a teachable moment: "The ears of all the people were attentive to the law." Ezra was wise enough, however, not simply to read out the Word of the Lord from the ancient text. He strategically placed no less than twenty six preachers throughout the crowd (most of them with multisyllable names that tangle the tongues of all but the most seasoned readers when this passage from Nehemiah, chapter 8, turns up once every three years in the Sunday eucharistic lectionary).

What did this small army of preachers do on this deeply solemn occasion? "They gave the sense, so that the people understood the reading."

Which of course, is what each of the preachers whose sermons we now hear in this section have, on analogously significant occasions, endeavored to do with their own congregations as well.

There's a Wideness in God's Mercy
(Requiem for Ann Bjorkman Taylor)

The Rev. Dayle Casey
The Chapel of Our Saviour
Colorado Springs, Colorado

Isaiah 25: 6-9
Psalm 40: 1-6
John 6: 37-39

∞

Five or six years before Ann Taylor was born, the infant son of President and Mrs. Kennedy died. And during the period of mourning, the president said, "It is against the laws of nature for a father to bury his son."

What I understood him to mean was that the death of a son or daughter is contrary to the way it's supposed to be. It's contrary to the way the world is supposed to work. *Why* such things happen is hard, if not impossible, for the human mind to comprehend and painful for the human heart to withstand.

This, of course, is equally true today . . . as we gather with Carol and Bill, and with Drake and Clay and Todd, to bury Ann, their daughter and sister and our friend and sister in Christ. And we come to ask God to help us in the midst of things we cannot understand.

I want to share with you three stories. They are stories about the way God helps us in the midst of things we cannot understand.

The first is the story of Jesus and the death of his friend Lazarus. Lazarus had fallen ill. No one knew why. There seemed to be no reason for it. And Mary and Martha, Lazarus' sisters, sent for Jesus to tell him that his friend was sick.

When Jesus arrived at Bethany, he found that Lazarus was already dead. And when he saw that Mary and those with her were weeping, "he was moved with compassion and was deeply distressed." "He groaned in his spirit," the Greek says literally, "agonized in the very heart of his being." And then, St. John (Chapter 11) says, "Jesus wept."

I don't think we make enough of this truth about Jesus: He wept at the death of a friend.

The truth about God that we find in Jesus is that God is one who *cares* for his creation, a God who comes to be with us in our sorrows as well as in our joys, in our weaknesses as well as in our strengths, a

God who took on human flesh that he might rejoice with those who rejoice and weep with those who weep.

As the hymn we're going to sing later reminds us,

> *There is no place where earth's sorrows*
> *are more felt than up in heaven;*
> *there is no place where earth's failings*
> *have such kindly judgment given.*

God helps us in the midst of things we cannot understand by sharing our pain. Jesus wept at the grave of his friend Lazarus. Just as surely, God himself wept at the cross, at the death of his own child—in the midst of things he himself was no doubt struggling to understand. It is no less certain that he weeps today with Bill and Carol and Drake and Todd and Clay and all the rest of us. God himself is moved at the very heart of his being when we are in pain.

But not only that. For several years God has wept with Ann, as well, in *her* sorrows and her pain, sorrows and pain many of you have known about but could not share as fully as God himself did, for there is no place where earth's sorrows are *more* felt than in heaven itself.

God helps us in the midst of things we cannot understand by caring for us, by caring enough to weep with us when we weep.

The second story is one Jesus himself told, a story we all know. At least, we have all *heard* it told, many times. Can we truly take it to ourselves and make it our own?

> *There once was a man who had two sons. And the younger son said to his father, "Father, give me my share of the property." So he divided his estate between them.*
>
> *A few days later the younger son turned the whole of his share into cash and left home for a distant country, where he lost every penny of it and had no more resources of his own. He had spent it all. He had nothing left, no more resources to see him through, and a severe famine fell upon that country and he began to be in need.*
>
> *So he went and attached himself to one of the local landowners, who sent him to his farm to mind the pigs. The young man would have been glad to fill his stomach with the pods the pigs were eating, but no one gave him anything.*
>
> *Then he came to his senses: "How many of my father's hired servants have more food than they can eat," he said. "And here I am starving to death!*

I will go at once to my father, and say to him, 'Father, I have sinned against God and against you; I am no longer fit to be called your son. Treat me as one of your hired servants.'"

So he set out for his father's house. But while he was still a long way off his father saw him . . . and his heart went out to him. And he ran to meet him, flung his arms around him, and kissed him.

We all remember the rest of the story . . . how the father would hear of nothing less than to take the best he had to dress and feast his son, for the one he loved had been lost and was found.

We remember the story. Do we believe it? Do we hold it dear to us in the very heart of our beings? The story is only secondarily about the son. It's more about our Father. Or, better, it's about the relationship that *endures* between us.

That father could not possibly have understood what took his son to a distant country. In fact, there is nothing in the story that suggests he even cared why his son was lost. It was just not the way it was supposed to be. Not a day passed that the father didn't go, in his mind and heart, in the very core of his being, to that distant country in search of his son, weeping for him, praying for him, agonizing over him.

Ann, we all know, was driven by something we do not understand to the distant land of chronic and painful depression. Time and again, she tried to escape, to return home, to be the joy to those who loved her that she had formerly been. But she could not.

Mother and father, brothers and friends, do not understand. They did not care *why* she was lost. All that mattered was that she was . . . and not a day passed that they didn't go, in mind and heart, in the very heart of their being, to that distant country in search of her, weeping for her, praying for her, agonizing over her.

Jesus once asked his disciples, "Would any of you offer your son or daughter a stone when they asked for bread? If you, then, mere human fathers and mothers that you are, know how to give good things to your children, how much more will your heavenly Father give good things to those who ask him?"

We do not understand, most of us, the distant country into which Ann was driven by her disease. But we do understand this—if we understand Jesus—that:

There's a wideness in God's mercy
like the wideness of the sea;
there's a kindness to his justice
which is more than liberty.
There is welcome for the sinner,
and more graces for the good;
there is mercy with the Savior;
there is healing in his blood.

We do not understand, most of us, the extent of the pain that Ann suffered. But we do understand this—if we understand Jesus—that:

There is no place where earth's sorrows
are more felt than up in heaven;
There is no place where earth's failings
have such kindly judgment given.
There is plentiful redemption
in the blood that has been shed;
There is joy for all the members
in the sorrows of the Head.

If you and I, mere human fathers and mothers that we are, know how to weep for our children when they weep, if we know how to pray for our children when they are lost and how to *run* to greet them when they return home, how much more will our heavenly Father give good things to his children when they return to him!

Gardner Taylor, the great Baptist preacher in Brooklyn, says that the whole of the Bible can be summed up this way—that God is out to get back what belongs to him. Or, to put another way, the Bible, from beginning to end, encourages us to trust God . . . to trust him in the midst of real life, even in the midst of those things, like today's things, that we cannot understand.

So we come today, not seeking easy answers, but seeking through our worship and our Eucharist to participate in and experience and trust the mystery that is life . . . and God. And to trust that it is good, even amidst the things we do not and perhaps cannot understand, remembering that:

The love of God is broader
than the measure of man's mind;
and the heart of the Eternal
is most wonderfully kind.
If our love were but more faithful,

we should take him at his word;
And our life would be thanksgiving
for the goodness of the word.

"Faith . . . hope . . . love . . ."—these three abide when all else changes or fails, St. Paul assures us. What are we human beings but a way God has of giving life to faith, to hope, and to love? And there simply are no easy explanations for these three abiding things. There is only the opportunity to *live* them within the mystery of the real life God has given us. There is only the opportunity to trust God even amidst the things we do not, and perhaps cannot, understand . . . and the opportunity to rejoice and give thanks to God for Ann, one of his own special gifts to us all.

Now. . . the third story:

There was a young man in a small town in France who took his own life. The young man's family, of course, were deeply distressed. When they met with the priest to plan their son's burial, they were even more greatly distressed to learn that because he had taken his own life, their son could not be buried in the consecrated grounds of the church cemetery. The priest said he was sorry, but the church's teachings did not permit it. Yet he did agree to bury the young man just outside the cemetery fence, as close to the consecrated grounds as possible.

The day for the burial came, and that's what they did. But during that night the priest could not sleep. He tossed and turned from the time he went to bed until the break of day. Then, getting the sexton up before breakfast, the priest went with the sexton to the cemetery with cedar posts and posthole diggers and moved the *fence* outside the grave.

Fences are the invention of man's mind. There are no fences round the kingdom of God, "for the love of God is broader than the measure of man's mind."

When his daughter Ann returned home last Friday night, her heavenly Father did not ask her where she had been or why she was back. While she was still a long way off he saw her, and his heart went out to her. And he ran to meet her, flung his arms around her, and kissed her. And he didn't have to open a gate to let her in. There are no fences round the kingdom of God.

> *For the love of God is broader*
> *than the measure of man's mind;*
> *and the heart of the Eternal*
> *is most wonderfully kind.*

Because of this, we *can* be more faithful, and take him at his *word;* and let our lives—even on this day—and throughout the years to come—be thanksgiving for the goodness of the Lord.

In the Name of God, Father, Son, and Holy Spirit. Amen.

It's Your Turn to Carry the Child

A Sermon by the Rev. Beth Wickenberg Ely
Christmas Eve, 1995
Preached at St. Patrick, Mooresville, and All Saints, Charlotte

Isaiah 9:2-4,6-7
Titus 2:11-14
Luke 2:1-20

∞

A funny thing happened to me this week when I went to get my hair cut. Kim, who is my stylist, is very pregnant, and, of course, we were discussing the due date of the baby. As other customers lined up behind me, she said to me in no uncertain terms, "Well, I'm not having this baby until after Christmas! There just isn't time." Several minutes later, just as she finished my hair, her water broke, and a few hours later she had a baby boy. Kim had her plans, and God had his plans.

A wonderful lead-in for tonight. Christmas Eve. The reason we are all here is because of the birth of a baby 2,000 years ago, a baby that came into the world as we all came into the world and as our own children came into the world—when he was ready, on someone else's divine timetable.

It couldn't have been very convenient for Mary to go into labor that night long ago. Of course, it wasn't convenient for the emperor, Caesar Augustus, back in Rome to call for a census near her due date, either. But the emperor was the emperor, and Mary and Joseph were just common folk in an occupied land. When the emperor said, "Go home to be registered," they went—to Joseph's people in Bethlehem because he was of King David's house. Mind you, it had been 1,000 years since David had ruled and he had thousands of descendants by then. Joseph, with his wife Mary, were only two—and plain people, after all.

They didn't even have enough money or influence to find a room in the crowded city. No doubt Mary, being like most women, had hoped that she would not have this child before she got back home to Nazareth. But she had not even had control over the conception of her child . . . the Holy Spirit had seen to that. So she, above everyone, knew that God's timetable was God's own.

Then as God would have it, while they were still in Bethlehem, her water broke and the time was near. It was darned inconvenient and probably pretty scary to go into labor in a strange place, so far from home. But they had to do the best they could. And so her son, whom she had been told to name Jesus, was born in a stable, probably a cave, with animals for company. She would have wanted better for him, but she had done all she could and she still could hold him close and love him and nurse him, even in a cave.

She had carried him in her womb, tenderly, protectively, this far. Now he was out into the world—God in the flesh. The Incarnation. Mary had done her job. She gave birth to the Son of God. That is what we join together to celebrate tonight.

That moment changed things for all time. It made everything different. God had so loved us that he took on our flesh, our vulnerability. God had never become a human being before. It was God's choice to be one of us. To be with us. Emmanuel. God with us. And in that moment—

> The unlimited chose to be limited.
> The infinite became finite.
> The unnameable became named.
> The unknowable became known.
> The undefined became defined.
> The wholly other became wholly present.
> The unapproachable became approachable.
> What had been eternally concealed was forever exposed.

Mary carried this gift of a Savior to that manger for us and gave him birth, in God's time. But also in a time in our history, on a certain date, on this earth, in the reign of Caesar Augustus, in a stable. In a moment in history, in one of our moments, just as this now is a moment, for us on Christmas Eve, far into our Christian history as a people.

One birth in the little town of Bethlehem, in an obscure place in a dominated country. Yet the story of what happened, beginning with the shepherds in the Gospel story tonight, has come to you and to me down through all these years.

Did we really listen to what St. Luke said about the shepherds?

Oh, we heard the part about their abiding in the fields keeping watch over their flocks by night. We know that the angel terrified them but told them to "fear not" and that she brought tidings of great joy for all the people. We know that once they heard about the babe, they hastily sought him out and came to worship him.

We see them in the creches each year, with Mary and Joseph and the baby and the requisite sheep and donkey and cow. Don't you have a sheep and a donkey and a cow in your manger scene at home? We have them here, too, in the manger scene in the church. The shepherds are here, worshiping, too. But what happens to them after that? They do not stay at the creche. Often we listeners of the Christmas story are lingering at this cozy manger scene and may not really hear what happened next.

Here's what the Gospel says: "When they saw this, they made known what had been told them about this child; and all who heard it were amazed at what the shepherds told them . . . The shepherds returned, glorifying and praising God for all they had heard and seen, as it had been told them."

We are heirs of those shepherds who carried the news. Still the story spreads abroad. Our children learn it from us, our grandchildren too. Old friends and new friends still need to hear the old story. Believers and unbelievers. The strangers in our midst. The seekers after meaning. All need to hear the good news that happened the first Christmas Eve: that God so loved the world that he gave his only begotten son.

Mary carried him there—to the manger. The shepherds carried him into the world. We are here together tonight because they carried him. We must carry him, too. And others that we teach will carry him, on down through history. This is no myth, no archetype. This is a real story about God who really came to be with us—Emmanuel.

Now let me tell you another story, a parable as told by Joseph P. Klock:

A small group of people were preparing to leave their country, which was under siege of war. They were being forced to travel over some of the most dangerous terrain in their country in order to escape. As they were about to leave, they were approached by a young woman who was carrying an infant and a frail old man who wanted to escape with them.

The leaders of the group agreed to take these frail refugees with them with the firm understanding that the men would carry the infant, but that the old man and the woman would have to make it on their own. All agreed to this plan.

Several days into their dangerous and grueling journey, the old man collapsed, saying that he was too exhausted to continue. He pleaded to be left behind to die in peace. They faced this harsh reality and decided that this was in fact what they would do.

Suddenly, the young mother walked up to the old man, knelt beside him and handed the infant to him. She told him that it was his turn to carry the child. She led the others as they walked away to continue their journey of escape. It was several moments before she paused to turn and look back. As she did, she saw the old man stumbling along the trail with the child in his arms.

Carry the child of Christmas, please. It's your turn to carry the child.

Amen.

This Is *Not* the Most Important Day of Your Life

The Rev. Meredith Woods Potter
Vicar, One in Christ Episcopal Church,
Park Ridge, Illinois, at time of delivery;
now Director of Academic Affairs, Seabury-Western Theological
Seminary

Sermon Preached at an Ordination to the Priesthood
Cathedral of St. James
Chicago, Illinois

Isaiah 6: 1-8
Psalm 138: 8-19
Philippians 4: 4-9
John 6: 35-38

∞

Excitement mixed with apprehension in her voice as the ordinand exclaimed, "This is going to be the most important day of my life!" I smiled, but I kept silent. One of the things I've learned is when not to embark upon a theological debate—or at least when to keep my mouth shut until a more propitious moment. But we do get our chances, and now seems as good a time as any for me to challenge that remark. And so I reply, quite simply and yet with conviction: "My beloved ordinands, today is not the most important day of your life!"

I discovered that astonishing reality in my own priesthood just twenty-three hours after I had been ordained. It was during my first celebration of the Holy Eucharist as a priest. I had just baptized two of my own grandchildren. And I heard myself say to them,

We receive you into the household of God. Confess the faith of Christ cruci-
fied, proclaim his resurrection, and share with us in his eternal priesthood.

And it was then that I realized that I, too, had been received into the household of God; I, too, had been charged to confess the faith of Christ crucified; I, too, had been anointed to proclaim Christ's resur-rection, and I had even been given a share in Christ's eternal priest-hood—but it hadn't been just the day before, on the Feast of St. Michael and All Angels in this cathedral in the year of our Lord 1985, the day I was ordained a priest. No, the most important day of my life had been on a day in 1934 in a much smaller church in Hyde Park when I, too, was sealed by the Holy Spirit in Baptism and marked as Christ's own forever.

And for each one of us gathered here today—ordinands, families, friends, loved ones—the most important day of each of our lives was our baptismal day. It was even on that day that we each received our ministries. And so what is happening today? What is the significance of today for you who are about to be ordained priest in the one, holy, catholic and apostolic church? If you were in fact given your ministry—your marching orders, so to speak—to confess the faith, to proclaim Christ's resurrection, and to share in his eternal priesthood on that day, then why are we gathered here today? What is the significance of this special call to you, the ordinands? What are you seven being set apart to do that you were not already called to do at your baptism?

In our first reading from Holy Scripture, God inquires, "Whom shall I send?" and the enthusiastic ordinand replies, "Here am I. Send me!" That passage is one of my favorites, but in a poignant sort of way, for it always reminds me of grade school. I was a very serious and enthusiastic student. And, frequently, I was the first to think I had the right answer. Up would go my hand, waving excitedly in the air. And if the teacher tried to call on anyone else, I would begin to jump up and down so as not to be overlooked. (I can tell by your response that the scene is not unfamiliar to some of you.) I would guess that some of you can sympathize with me and my childhood frustration. But I would suspect that others of you recollect a different frustration—a frustration of not getting called on because someone like me volunteered too often; of not having time to figure out the answer because someone like me responded too quickly; of not feeling a part of the class because someone like me seemed to be playing a private game of "ask and tell" with the teacher.

Now, at long last, when I hear that passage read, I hear God saying, "Sit down, Meredith. I know you're there. I have my own plans for you. Let's get someone else to respond today." And that, my dear friends, is what I believe to be at the very heart of the priesthood—to encourage others to respond to God's call to them; to encourage all the baptized who will be put in your charge to exercise their own ministries; to equip the faithful—the shy faithful—to confess their faith; to teach others how to proclaim the resurrection. For you are being given the precious gift of helping to empower others to share with you in Christ's eternal priesthood.

How, then, do those of us called to the priesthood carry out such an awesome task? I think that it begins with our own spiritual lives. I've learned that the most important spiritual life for which I as a priest am responsible is my own. It all boils down to the fact that I can't preach what I don't practice. I cannot convince unless I am convinced; I cannot compel unless I am compelled; and I cannot kindle the fire of the Holy Spirit in others if my own light is not burning strongly.

If the only time we priests read Holy Scripture is when we are preparing a sermon or an adult education class, then when do we hear God speaking to us? If our prayer time is consumed with the petitions of those who have requested our prayers, then when do we enter into the deeper relationship of prayer that begins with our own adoration and praise, our own thanksgiving, our own repentance, our own listening to God? One of my dearest friends and colleagues once said to me, "My work is my prayer." Wrong! Our prayer is our work.

It is interesting to note that in Paul's letter to the Philippians, he says to keep on doing the things that we have learned and received and heard. I hear that to mean that the first task of the priest is to keep on doing faithfully those things we learned about the Christian life and first began to practice as baptized members of the church. For example, most Wednesday mornings at 7:00 A.M. you will find me attending the Holy Eucharist in a neighboring church. Attending a midweek service was part of my personal rule of life for many years before I was ordained, and it has more meaning and importance to me now than ever. For it is there that I hear the words of the Great Thanksgiving very differently than when I'm saying them; it is there that I worship with a community for which I am not personally responsible; it is there that I find refreshment.

Going on retreats, seeing my spiritual director regularly, meeting weekly with my small group were part of my rule of life as a lay person, and these same practices now sustain me as a priest. One thing in my life did change quite radically, however. I always tried to keep the Sabbath as a day of rest; and now I work on Sundays. When I was first ordained, the other priests who serve Korean congregations warned me against taking a day off. Their rationale was that since most immigrants work seven days a week, priests would be thought lazy if they worked any less. I didn't take their advice. In fact I chose to make quite public what day of the week I was taking off. Now, ten years later, more than half of my congregation has followed suit. They close their stores on Sunday so that they, too, can have a day of rest. We preach most convincingly what we practice most consistently.

In today's Gospel Jesus says, "I am the bread of life. Whoever comes to me will never be hungry, and whoever believes in me will never be thirsty." Every single baptized Christian here today is called to live those words. But now you who are about to be ordained are being called to live those words as you have never lived them before. Because, now, as you live those words, you will invite, bring, and sometimes carry others into the reality that those words hold for your life.

And so go forth to proclaim by word and deed the good news of Christ Jesus. Preach Christ's forgiveness; pronounce God's blessing; nourish and nurture Christ's people. And remember that from this day forward you will be leading others into the most important day of their lives.

**Good News for Failed Saints
(All Saints' Day)**

Sermon preached by
The Reverend William J. Eakins
November 5, 1995
All Saints Sunday
Trinity Episcopal Church
Hartford, Connecticut

St. Matthew 5: 1-12

∞

Have you ever had the experience of meeting a famous person in the flesh? I think probably the most famous person I've ever met is Queen Elizabeth of England. Her majesty visited my college at Oxford when I was an undergraduate, and, as senior Bible Clerk, I was asked to say the college's Latin grace at dinner. Along with several other junior members of the college, I thus had the honor of being presented to the queen. It was a very impressive occasion. I remember being struck with the queen's great dignity, her natural assumption of respect. On the other hand, I shall always remember how that, for all her regalness, the queen was nonetheless very obviously a human being. In fact, I was struck by how very short she was; I felt as if I towered over her. Also, I could not help noticing those little telltale signs of advancing age, especially the worry lines on her forehead.

I wonder if surprise such as mine at finding out that a famous person like Queen Elizabeth is, after all, a mere mortal like ourselves is not akin to the difficulty we have in comprehending that the saints of God are, as the familiar hymn puts it, "just folk like me." The root of our difficulty lies, I think, in our understanding of what constitutes holiness. What does it mean for a person to be holy?

I suggest that the answer most of us would give to that question would probably interpret holiness largely in terms of perfection. A holy person is one whose whole being—mind, heart, and spirit—is dedicated to God. Or we might say that a holy person is one in whom all the qualities that we know are of God—love, joy, peace, patience, wisdom, and the like—dwell in full measure. If, then, saints are holy people (and that by definition is true), then if you and I were to aspire to sainthood we would have to become infinitely better people than we know ourselves to be. Our minds, which are full of such a hodgepodge of thoughts of all kinds about such things as checking accounts, loved ones, enemies, jobs, romance, and vacations, would have to undergo a thorough housecleaning so that they could be taken over with thoughts of God alone. Our hearts, which we know are full of all kinds of feelings—from love to lust, hope to hate—would have to undergo a powerful purge in order to be filled only with fine, noble, and godly feelings. No wonder we give up in despair when we consider the transformation that would have to take place within us for us to clean up our act and become anything like the perfect people God wants us to be.

If sainthood, holiness, means perfection or near perfection, no wonder it is so hard for us to believe that saints are "just folk like me." Sainthood must be for people very different from you and me, the few people whose character has reached such a state of perfection that they live very close to God, far closer than we could ever hope to live.

Let all of us failed "saints" turn, however, to this morning's Gospel reading and listen carefully and thankfully to the good news it contains. The Beatitudes that we hear this morning, coming from the lips of the man we call God's Anointed One, confront us with a startlingly different picture of what it means for us to be holy. If you think living close to God means having your spiritual life all put together so that you are living in a state of complete contentment and unalloyed peace and joy, listen to what Jesus says.

"Blessed are you who are poor, for yours is the kingdom of God." Now maybe you are thinking, "Well, that leaves me out, I've really got enough to live on even though I have to be careful about how I spend my money." What about your inner life, however? What about the life of your soul? Do you feel rich, having all you could possibly need, thank you very much? Or do you feel as though there is much that is lacking, that there are many areas in which you fall far short of what God expects? If you feel like a spiritual pauper, hear the good news: You are blessed, yours is the kingdom of God. And why is that? Because God is about the business of saving sinners and not cosseting the righteous. It is those who are keenly aware of their shortcomings who are closest to God because they know how much they need God's mercy. On the other hand, the spiritually rich who think they have all they need find their consolation in their own goodness and cut themselves off from the riches of God's love.

"Blessed are you who are hungry now, for you will be filled." Perhaps you think, "That can't mean me because I have plenty to eat, so much so that I have to be careful of eating too much." But what about the spirit within you? Are you filled with contentment? Or do you sometimes feel "like a motherless child, a long way from home"? If you do, listen to the good news: "Blessed are you," Jesus says. Blessed are you, because it is those who seek who shall find; it is to those who knock that the door will be opened; it is those who know they are hungry that God can fill. On the other hand, it is those who are satisfied, who do *not* hunger and thirst after righteousness, whom God finds it very difficult if not impossible to nourish.

"Blessed are you that weep now, for you shall laugh." Do you ever weep for yourself, for things done and left undone, for that which might have been but will now never be? Do you ever weep for the ones you love as you think of their pain and long for their well-being? Do you ever weep for the world as you remember the violence and the suffering that plague humanity? If the tears ever flow and the heart ever breaks, Jesus says, "Blessed are you." Blessed are you, because the tears of contrition and the broken heart of compassion bring us very close to God, the God who in love weeps for the waywardness of the world God made and for all of us, God's children. Those who weep draw near to the heart of the mystery that is God; those who are strangers to sorrow are strangers to God.

"Blessed are you when people hate you, and when they exclude you, revile you, and defame you on account of the Son of Man." We might expect that the sign of being blessed by God would be success in life and the enjoyment of the admiration of our friends and colleagues. Jesus, however, tells us something quite different. Blessedness consists not in success but in the trying to do what is right, not in the enjoyment of the praise of others but of the praise of God. There is many a person who in human eyes may appear to have it made who in God's eyes is an utter failure. Likewise, there are many who are failures in human eyes who in God's sight are heroes.

I thus hear the Beatitudes of this morning's Gospel reading holding up a very different idea of what it means to be a holy person, what it means to be a saint. It is an idea of personal holiness that means not perfection but an awareness of brokenness and an earnest, humble striving to be made whole, seeking no reward other than that of God's "Servant, well done." If we believe what Jesus tells us to be true, then sainthood is not some unattainable goal, the preserve of the unnaturally, super-humanly good. Rather, sainthood is indeed the calling that is close at hand to all of us, because it consists not of our goodness but rather our willingness to be open to the goodness of God.

I love this observation by Phyllis McGinley:

> *The wonderful thing about saints is that they were human. They lost their tempers, scolded God, were egotistical or testy or impatient in their turns, made mistakes and regretted them. Still they went on doggedly blundering toward heaven.*

It is to that sort of sainthood that I hear Jesus calling us in this morning's Gospel. So, dear friends and fellow saints, let us doggedly blunder on. Heaven awaits not the perfect but sinners in need of salvation.

Mystery Loves Company
Mitties McDonald De Champlain
Associate Professor of Preaching and Communication Studies
Fuller Theological Seminary

Genesis 1: 1-2: 3
2 Corinthians 13: (5-10) 11-14
Matthew 28: 16-20
Trinity Sunday

∞

When I first came to Fuller Seminary eleven years ago, one of my first off-campus experiences was to conduct a series of workshops for Episcopal clergy in the Diocese of Los Angeles along with one of my colleagues—also an Episcopal priest—in the Preaching Department. My senior colleague had selected the following title for the workshops: "The Majesty, Mystery and Misery of Preaching." He dealt with the majesty and mystery—which is to say the theology—in his presentations. And I, of course, as the so-called communication expert, dealt with the misery of preaching.

It was my task, actually, using the received wisdom of communication theory, to help reduce what I have come to call the Misery Index of preaching—which is the combined frustration of exegetical preparation and delivery. And I continue to this day to deal in my classes with the Misery Index. But you see, I also have a Misery Index, and my personal index skyrocketed off the charts yesterday afternoon shortly after being greeted by Dian Alling here at Cotterman Hall. She said in passing, "I look forward to hearing you preach tomorrow." I said, somewhat nervously I suppose, "Oh thanks." At which point someone else—I think—chimed in, "When was the last time you heard a good sermon on the Trinity?" Dian's response was swift: "I've never heard a good sermon on the Trinity—except when Roger Alling preached on it." Everyone broke into immediate laughter, and I laughed too, of course. But my "still small voice of calm" did begin temporarily to hear my still small voice of panic becoming especially vocal as the afternoon progressed.

And then my partner faculty member in our small group last night said, "Surely, as a seminary professor you'll have something to say in your sermon on the Trinity." And my still small voice of panic now had its own special line of immediate reply from within, furnished courtesy of Roger Alling's opening sermon to us: "Well, I *have* to *say something.*"

The gentle teasing of yesterday afternoon made me realize that the Misery Index of preachers everywhere goes sky high on occasions like Trinity Sunday. I assume the reason for this is that the doctrine is so big—so mysterious—that it defies easy or obvious assembly of sermons about it. And we, of course, live in an age that is so pragmatic and so obsessed with information processing and control that the doctrine of the Trinity is just too remote a thing. One really has to be a card carrying "mystic" for the pulse to quicken on Trinity Sunday. As one church analyst keenly observed, "The mystics are out of fashion; the most appealing forms of religion in the early nineties are those which offer certainty rather than mystery." Nevertheless, the holy fact remains that the Trinity is at the very heart of Christian self-understanding: one God in three Persons: Father, Son, and Holy Spirit—coeternally and coequally God; not three Gods; not three modes of God.

There is nothing I can explain to you about the Trinity that you haven't already learned full well in your systematic theology courses to date. But we all must reaffirm the importance of this doctrine to our common life. And so I would like to invite you to live into the mystery of the Holy Trinity today by hearing again the words of Jesus to his disciples:

> *All authority in heaven and on earth has been given to me. Go therefore and make disciples of all nations, baptizing them in the name of the Father and of the Son and of the Holy Spirit, and teaching them to obey everything that I have commanded you. And remember, I am with you always, to the end of the age.*

The experience of the risen and glorified Jesus was a mystery in and of itself to those first disciples: "They worshiped him," says Matthew. "But some doubted." You see, mystics were out of fashion even in the first century. And besides, the disciples were probably already worrying, "How on earth are we going to preach this? How will we be able to make it credible, intelligible, convincing to a world of first-century skeptics?" If we twentieth century folk find this Trinitarian reference in Matthew hard to cope with after nearly two thousand years of theological reflection, imagine how those first disciples must have felt abut this "Mystery of the Ages" revealed to them in the coming of Christ—God with us—to earth. Imagine their Misery Index in those early days, because Jesus remained in many ways a mystery to them to the end.

Forget the Misery Index for a moment. If I were to distill into a single phrase what this Gospel lesson points to about our Triune God, it would go like this: *Mystery loves company*. I repeat: Mystery *loves* company. Our God, as we know well, is essentially a God of communion and embrace. Everything in our liturgies points to this; we reenact this holy mystery every time we make Eucharist together—Holy Communion. All of us are indebted to our fourth-century brother, St. Basil the Great, who was the first to speak of the Trinity as being made up of three Persons and one Communion—Father, Son, and Holy Spirit—who share a common will and purpose.

What this means is that we do well always to remember that our God is a God of right relationship. And as our Genesis passage affirms this morning, God created everything that is—cattle and creeping things and wild animals and you and me because *Mystery loves company*. James Weldon Johnson captured the mystery well when he said in his poem:

> *And God stepped out on space,*
> *And He looked around and said,*
> *"I'm lonely—*
> *I'll make me a world."*

The very movement of God intended in the whole of creation is a movement toward union, communion, connectedness, relationship. And we humans, above all, are made in the Divine Image to be in right relationship with God and with one another. *Mystery loves company.* Douglas John Hall gives a most beautiful reflection on all this when he says, "We move toward real humanity, not when we have achieved all manner of personal successes of brain, will, or body, but when through the media of brain, will, and body we have entered as unreservedly as possible into communion with 'the other'."

And, of course, our God in Trinity establishes communion with us for all time and eternity in the Sacrament of Baptism. *Mystery loves company.* Holy Mystery wants to be bound to us. I can only assume that is what our Prayer Book is driving at when it declares: "The bond which God establishes in Baptism is indissoluble." We are incorporated into the very life of God in Trinity and become creatures in full communion with God in our Baptism—marked as Christ's own forever. I love the observation of the theologian who noted that "true religion is the original umbilical cord that binds our individual selves back to God." The image of the umbilical cord is for me a wonderfully resonant image, because it points so beautifully to our need for total dependence on God for all our nurture. God in Trinity is our true and universal source of being, and it is in baptism that we are bound with a cord that cannot be broken.

Still, we remain creatures who are bound to have trouble in our Christian lives and in our preaching lives. So we are empowered through the Eucharist to keep our communion with God flourishing and to make our communion with each other authentic and abundant. God makes eucharist with us as a means of grace and a vehicle of eternal charity. *Mystery loves company.* And we gather week after week to "join our voices with Angels and Archangels and with all the company of heaven" to reaffirm our belief that God is eternally present with us, for us, by us, in us . . . to reaffirm that we long to live together in unity, constancy, and peace.

Mystery loves company. And it is by faith with thanksgiving that we *eat* and live and *preach* into that mystery, confident that the "grace of the Lord Jesus Christ, the love of God, and the communion of the Holy Spirit" are with us always. So breathe on us breath of God; bind us together in your truth.

"GLORIFY THE LORD, ALL YOU WORKS OF THE LORD"
THE VOICE OF THE SPIRIT IN THE FORCES OF CULTURE

NOTHING TAKES PLACE IN THE WORLD OUTSIDE THE CHURCH, the sounds of which do not seep in under the doors and into the sanctuary. The challenge for the preacher is how to honor these voices appropriately.

Some of these voices have a conversation-enriching potential that is both obvious and welcome. Who, for instance, would begrudge sharing the pulpit with a powerful preaching colleague like the poet George Herbert? **Thomas Troeger,** himself a poet and a teacher of preaching, gives Herbert's voice a contemporary hearing in conversation with his own life experience, and with the word of Jesus in John, chapter 14.

Some cultural voices are more current than Herbert's, and more cacophonous as well—voices of anguish or anger, voices that pose a strident and frightening threat to the very conversation into which they insistently demand an entry. What happens, when, on the Second Sunday of Easter, the Alleluia trumpets are drowned out in the roar of a bomb blast that destroys the Federal Building in Oklahoma City? With the support of another literary artist, Boris Pasternak, preacher **James Law**—himself a pastor in Oklahoma City, struggles to respond with honesty and hope in the midst of this most difficult Sunday.

And what is to be done with other anxious voices, voices that are not nearly so shrill, but which hang around whining and just won't go away—voices that have become so common, they are in danger of being relegated to the status of annoying background noise?

Marriage. In spite of all the sentimental hype that surrounds it, is marriage a doomed and dying institution in our society? Does the Word of God have anything to offer those who marry, other than pious platitudes and moralistic pronouncements—which the church often asserts as absolutes—and which culture all but universally ignores? **Jonathan Currier**, realizing that practical theological teaching and sensitive pastoral support for marriage must be wider, deeper, and bolder than what can be measured out in short wedding homilies, undertakes substantive marriage catechesis in a Sunday morning sermon.

What kind of credentials can validate one's existence and prove one's worth? Homiletics professor **William Hethcock** knows that soon-to-be priests are not immune to the tensions in such nagging questions. A priest himself, Hethcock also knows that those approaching Holy Orders may be especially vulnerable to the pervasive cultural pressure for credentials. So he plays out the struggle of the apostle Paul, who also has to contend with a "prove you have earned the right to our attention" dynamic that is blatant in the adolescent spirituality of the Galatian church.

Can't we put our trust in *anything* that is solid, certain, and secure? Are not our religious beliefs at least *one* secure hiding place from the ambiguities inherent in a secular, pluralistic culture? **Donald Waring** takes on that set of questions with the help of such unlikely sermon conversation partners as St. Paul, Abraham, Dostoyevsky, and the Grand Inquisitor in *The Brothers Karamazov*.

And then there are other voices in our culture—soft and gentle ones that can provide rich nourishment and stimulate healthy growth, but only if some preacher makes a special effort to listen for their quiet murmur beneath other, louder voices. **Joy Rogers** has done such listening and invites her congregation to lean in close and catch the subtle sounds of "the little tradition" that lives in the homey, earthy parables of a Jewish carpenter and in the rituals of Scottish midwives and watching women.

Culture is, of course, an umbrella term for a multitude of different kinds of voices. Depending on which voice is speaking and what it sounds like, the preacher may decide that "culture" must be stood against, affirmed and blessed, risen above, held in tension with the gospel, or transformed by the gospel in the sermon proclamation to be shaped and shared with a faith community. (The alternatives are those suggested by H. Richard Niebuhr in his classic work, *Christ and Culture*.) Different preachers in different situations may see the homiletical task of addressing culture in widely varying, sometimes in radically conflicting, ways.

One thing, however, is quite clear: the many voices of culture cannot be ignored in the preaching conversation—not just because they will demand a hearing, but also because they have a legitimate and essential place at the table. These voices too are vehicles for the voice of the Spirit. Prophets in every generation continue to bear witness to *that* Spirit witness, even though the precise meaning of the Spirit's leading may be difficult to discern, and (at times) impossible to agree upon.

In the sermons gathered for this section, each preacher undertakes the risky task of welcoming a cultural voice that he or she has distinctively heard; and, trusting in the Spirit's promise to lead its listeners into all truth, each preacher has artfully orchestrated that cultural voice in the sermon conversation for the challenge, healing, and uplifting of the church.

Come My Way, My Truth, My Life

A Sermon by Professor Thomas Troeger,
Ralph E. and Norma E. Peck Professor
of Preaching and Communications, Iliff School of Theology,
Denver, Colorado
Campus for the Anglican Studies Program in Denver

∞

"Come, my Way, my Truth, my Life: such a way as gives us breath; such a truth as ends all strife; such a life as killeth death.

Come, my Light, my Feast, my Strength: such a light as shows a feast; such a feast as mends in length; such a strength as makes his guest.

Come, my Joy, my Love, my Heart: such a joy as none can move; such a love as none can part; such a heart as joys in love."

(The sermon explores this poem by George Herbert, found in the Hymnal, 1982, # 487.)

The poem draws on John 14:6, Jesus' words: "I am the way, and the truth, and the life. No one comes to the Father except through me." Notice how Herbert transforms the biblical verse. The poet personalizes it. In the Gospel of John, Jesus describes himself as *the* way, *the* truth, *the* life. But Herbert invokes Christ as *my* way, *my* truth, *my* life.

The poem gives witness to an essential insight about religious belief: the power of faith is never fully manifest until it becomes personally true in our own lives. It is when something becomes true for us in the core of our heart, that it changes us, that it mobilizes our energies to act and speak and live in a distinctive way. Personal truth is much more gripping than truth in the abstract. It is one thing to have general ideas about child rearing. It is an entirely other thing to be a parent.

It is one thing to have general ideas about how to deal with pain and suffering. It is an entirely other thing to see someone you love die a slow, agonizing death.

It is one thing to have general ideas about how to change society. It is an entirely other thing to try to get a piece of decent legislation passed.

It is one thing to have general ideas about Jesus Christ, to read in an ancient Gospel that he is the way, the truth, the life. It is an entirely other thing to call upon him as my way, my truth, my life.

Religion is no longer a chess game in the mind. It is how I live and act and speak day by day. How I treat my neighbor. How I seek reconciliation with my enemy. How I work for justice. How I pray with urgent, heartfelt intensity: Come, *my Way, my Truth, my Life:* Come, *my Light, my Feast, my Strength:* Come, *my Joy, my Love, my Heart.*

When Herbert prays, he is not seeking some vague spiritual experience. He names the tangible impact of Christ on our lives.

> *Come, my Way, my Truth, my Life:*
> *Such a way, as gives us breath:*
> *Such a truth, as ends all strife:*
> *And such a life, as killeth death.*
>
> *Such a way, as gives us breath.*

Perhaps the line means: come into our life by giving us the Spirit. For breath is often equated with the Spirit. And in the Gospel of John, Christ breathes the Spirit upon the disciples.

But the line *Such a way, as gives us breath* might also mean quite literally: come as the very source of breath, the inhaling and exhaling of my lungs. For Christ is the Word through whom all things were made. And when that Word becomes personal for us, when Christ becomes my way, when Christ becomes your way, then there is a heightened sense of how our breath and pulse are a gift that we have done nothing to earn.

I recall a time when I had a heightened sense of how breath and pulse are gifts from God. I was in a hospital intensive care unit recovering from surgery to replace my aortic valve with a mechanical one. Unfortunately, my bed was next to a heating vent that had a banging flap. I prayed to God, "Please silence that vent so I can sleep." Then all of a sudden I realized it was not the heating vent. It was my new mechanical heart valve. "Cancel that prayer, God."

But ever since then I have awakened every morning praying, "Thank you, God, my heart is beating. Thank you, God, my lungs are breathing."

Have you ever thought of this: how second by second you are receiving the gift of pulse and breath? Take your hand and open and close it like this. Keep at it. Pretend it is your heart. It if is an average heart, it may do this 70 times a minute, 4,200 times an hour, 32,000 times in the course of the night.

Have you ever received a utility bill for your pulse beat and your lungs breathing? Have you gotten a notice, "You are behind in your payments for pulse and breath, so we are shutting off service"?

Such a way, as gives us breath is a way that makes us aware that our breath is a gift. Instead of griping about all that we lack, we start giving thanks. We realize that to exist is to receive gift upon gift every second that we live.

> *Come, my Way, my Truth, my Life:*
> *Such a way, as gives us breath:*
> *Such a truth, as ends all strife.*

What kind of truth ends all strife? Is it the truth of some sacred text or creed? Judging from the way religious people have tortured and killed and accused each other of heresy over different interpretations of sacred texts, I can only conclude, No, the truth that ends all strife is not a sacred text.

Is it some scientific truth, a law of nature empirically tested and verified? Judging from our capacity to use our scientific knowledge for destructive and violent ends, I can only conclude, No, the truth that ends all strife is not a scientific truth.

Not a sacred text. Not a scientific law. The truth that ends all strife is Christ, the living embodiment of God's peace, God's wholeness, God's shalom.

If we look at this broken world, if we consider all the grief and alienation that have marked our own lives, then many of us would say we have known precious little of *such a truth, as ends all strife.*

And yet I have had glimpses of such a truth, momentary and fleeting though they have been.

I think of a colleague. Bitter disagreement had separated us. My colleague took the initiative to come to me. He spoke. Then I spoke. Sentence by sentence, we exchanged verbal snapshots of each other's world. We gave up trying to change each other. We settled for understanding each other. Alienation gave way to respect. And when my colleague left, we shook hands and said to each other, "Grace and peace." And for a moment, a brief moment that had the quality of eternity about it, we knew *such a truth, as ends all strife.*

> *Come, my Way, my Truth, my Life:*
> *Such a way, as gives us breath:*
> *Such a truth, as ends all strife:*
> *And such a life, as killeth death.*

What kind of life has the power to kill death? It is usually death that is killing life. A life that is not haunted by the fear of death is *such a life, as killeth death*. For the worst of death is not death itself but our fear of it.

Several years ago there was a priest in Uganda who, during the reign of the ruthless dictator Idi Amin, faced death at the hands of his henchmen.

The assassins showed up one day in the vestry of the priest's church. They told him they were going to shoot him right there on the spot. They asked the priest if he had anything to say before he died. He told the assassins that he was alive in Christ and that they were already dead in their sin. Then he said that after they shot him and he came into the full presence of Christ, he would pray for them.

The priest shut his eyes and waited for the rain of bullets.

Nothing happened.

He opened his eyes. They put down their guns, and they asked if the priest would pray for them now, here on earth. Yes, of course he would. They shut their eyes. The priest, as he acknowledges in his account of the story, kept his eyes open and prayed for the men who had come to kill him. Not only did they not shoot the priest, many of them became part of the resistance, helping people to escape assassination: *Such a Life, as killeth death*.

> Come, my Way, my Truth, my Life:
> Such a way, as gives us breath:
> Such a truth, as ends all strife:
> And such a life, as killeth death.

Imagine what it would mean if the poet's prayer became our prayer. Imagine how much change that might bring in us, in the world. If the poet's prayer became our prayer, we would know every breath is a gift from God.

Imagine what that would do to the greed that feeds our plunder of the environment. If the poet's prayer became our prayer, we would see the world through the eyes of our enemies.

Imagine what that would do to the bitterness that feeds our conflict and violence. If the poet's prayer became our prayer, we would live unhaunted by the fear of death.

Imagine what that would do to our cowardice in the face of injustice. If the poet's prayer became our prayer, there would be a profound change in us, the kind of change that empowers us to change the world.

Change this profound does not happen once and for all time. Change this profound has to be nurtured. Change this profound requires that we pray for Christ to feed us, for Christ to be our joy and our love.

And so today we join with George Herbert and offer the poet's prayer as our own prayer:

> *Come, my Light, my Feast, my Strength:*
> *Such a light, as shows a feast:*
> *Such a feast, as mends in length:*
> *Such a strength, as makes his guest.*
>
> *Come, my Joy, my Love, my Heart:*
> *Such a joy, as none can move:*
> *Such a love, as none can part:*
> *Such a heart, as joys in love.*
>
> *Copyright, 1996. Thomas H. Troeger, used by permission*

Burying the Dead in the Kingdom of God

Sermon by The Reverend James W. Law
April 23, 1995, The Second Sunday of Easter
Four Days After the Bombing of Oklahoma City Federal Building

∞

Boris Pasternak wrote, "Everything that happens in the world takes place not only on the earth that buries the dead, but also in some other dimension which some call the Kingdom of God."

We have all spent the past four days "on the earth that buries the dead." Four days of hell and horror, and apparently not soon to be over. Four days none of us will ever forget, for they are indelibly imprinted in our minds and in our memories.

Someone said to me this past week, "Father Law, what kind of world is this, anyway?" And I replied, with a flash of insight not my own, "It's the same kind of world it's always been." It is the world as old as Cain who killed his brother Abel. It's the world that gave us Joseph Stalin and Adolf Hitler, and that's the ugly side of the world that has been given to us. But we must never forget that the same world has also given us Moses and Jesus, Albert Schweitzer and Mother Teresa.

The world is a mixture, the world is a combination of good and evil, and this past week we have looked into the dark side of reality. It has become clear, I think, to each and every one of us that our primary relationship with reality is one of belonging and involvement. Our relationship with reality is not of distance and detachment. No, indeed we are part of what we see, and we are connected to what we see, and we cannot escape that. There is not one of us who has not felt himself or herself to be, at one point or another this week, downtown, whether we were physically there or not. Last Wednesday, reality forced itself on us in a horrifyingly ugly way. Wednesday, reality came to us as darkness, tragedy, as evil and wickedness. It turned our world upside down, and that inversion has left us confused and bewildered, not to mention outraged and angry.

The dark side of creation, the dark side of reality, has forced itself into our lives with an intrusion of colossal proportions. We have looked into the face of evil and found it ugly beyond description, horrifying beyond words. We remember the words that Jeremiah spoke to us years and years and years ago: the human heart "is deceitful above all things, and desperately wicked." And, too sadly, we have discovered or rediscovered the agonizing truth of those words.

But darkness is not all there is. The earth that buries its dead is not all there is. There is another dimension to reality, another dimension to human existence that is very, very different indeed. "Come ye blessed of my father," said Jesus, "inherit the kingdom prepared for you from the foundation of the world, because I was hungry and you fed me, I was thirsty and you gave me a drink, I was a stranger and you took me in, naked and you clothed me, sick and you visited me, in prison and you came unto me."

There is that level of reality also, and we are witnesses of these things this past week. We have seen the best that humankind can offer come to the fore. Not one of us has been left untouched by the courage of the fire fighters, the police, the rescue workers. Not one of us has been left untouched by the dedication, the commitment, of the medical personnel and all the volunteers who have given of themselves so readily and so unstintingly. They have shown us the beauty, the beauty of reality. They have shown us reality as God intends it to be. Reality where man loves man, and brother and sister, arm in arm, reach out in love, regardless of personal danger, and they do so just because they know that's the way things ought to be. That's the way we ought to behave and react toward each other.

I envy you Oklahomans. There is a part in me that is terribly, terribly humbled by you, because you have shown the world how to love, you have shown the world how to care for each other, you have shown the world what it means to lay down your lives for each other. You ought to be proud. Proud in a very humbling sense of that word—not prideful but proudful. Proudful of your brothers and sisters, your brother Okies and your sister Sooners, names that will forever be held in awe and wonder, not derision. The world has seen the best humanity has to offer, the world has seen the best through you.

You have brought tears, tears of sadness but tears of joy to the eyes of people all across this globe through your courage and your self-sacrificing love, your commitment to your fellow human beings, your quiet deeds of heroism. Think for a moment, not simply of the fire fighters and the rescue workers, but think of those ordinary, everyday people like you and me who stood for hours and hours in line to give a pint of blood, just because someone needed a pint of blood. It is incredible, all these examples to the whole world of what it means to be a human being, of what it means to be a creature created in the image of God.

No, I don't pretend to understand the darkness that haunts God's creation. I don't pretend to understand, because I can't, the suffering and pain that seems so central to human existence. I can't give you a systematic analysis of evil, because the face of evil wears many masks. But neither, I fear, can I give you a detailed analysis of goodness. I cannot delineate for you the component parts of the joys of love and the importance and happiness of family or what it means to be a community united together, united together in love. And I can't do those things because love's image must be seen to be felt, or felt to be seen.

Perhaps the picture of the policeman passing the baby to the fireman comes closest to showing us an image of the earth that buries the dead, also at the same time, that other dimension that some call the kingdom of God. In that picture we see in the midst of unspeakable horror such tenderness and such gentleness, such care and concern, such love and devotion. In the midst of horror, that picture ought to remind us that God himself is in the middle of life.

Our task, it seems to me, is to see in that picture the image of Christ and to feel and perceive the tears of the weeping Christ as he laments his hurt children and his broken brothers and sisters. People hurt and Christ dies, and God somehow is as much a victim of evil as we are. That is what the crucifixion is all about: that in Christ God himself went to the cross, that in Christ God himself suffered, that in Oklahoma City Christ suffers, and God suffers. God is in the middle of life, and Christ trudges with us to all of our personal Calvarys, large and small. In all of our tragedies and all of our heartbreaks, all of this senseless loss of human life, Christ is with us, because he is a part of this world that buries the dead, and of that other dimension some call the kingdom of God.

In the name of the Father, and of the Son, and of the Holy Ghost. Amen.

We Have Each Other for Healing

Sermon for the Fifth Sunday of Easter, Year B
The Rev. Jonathan E. Currier

∞

It wasn't an auspicious beginning. John had had a hard time making the commitment. Sure we'll get married, he kept saying, but the proposal never came. Finally, after a four-year courtship, Mary put her foot down. Marry me or I'll break it off, she said, and she went out the next Saturday with a young clerk in her office who had been asking for a date for weeks, just to give him something to think about. It made him think, and a few days later he did propose. Three months later they heard themselves say "I do" in the church where she had grown up.

This was a ways back; they hadn't slept together before, so the wedding night was a bit awkward, even difficult. He was more than a little anxious, and she kept thinking it was somehow her fault, that she wasn't attractive or alluring enough. It wasn't much better several weeks later, and hurtful words were exchanged, tears shed. Yet love and hope persisted, and they managed somehow that year to coax each other into the comfort and worship of each other's body.

There were turf battles aplenty those first few years. Who takes out the trash, how the toothpaste tube is squeezed, how long the dishes can go unwashed: all these seemingly minor issues, and many more, loomed ever larger in importance. Negotiations over the issues proved fractious. There were enough slammed doors and raised voices to prompt their elderly neighbors to come by a couple of times to inquire politely whether "everything was all right." Yet over time a domestic geography was mapped, with boundaries that would shift a little over their lives, but not too much. Eventually he stopped forgetting to put out the trash, started washing his dirty dishes right after he ate. She started squeezing the toothpaste tube from the bottom, though she never understood why she needed to, and she learned too that complaints about lapses were best left until after the morning coffee. Concessions had to be made. Once they became ingrained as habit, it became hard to understand why getting there had been so hard.

In their fifth year of marriage, a baby arrived, a little boy. They had been trying and praying for a child for three years. He was a dream come true. But two months later the child died in his sleep, a victim of SIDS. They were devastated. She took it as some strange judgment

from God and fell into a deep depression. She became cold, phleg-
matic. He tried to share her grief, but she wouldn't let him in.
Eventually he became angry. What about his grief, his pain? he
thought. She's not the only one who is suffering. In a fury one night,
he stormed out of the house and ended up spending the week at his
brother's place. But he called her every night, and when he went home
he decided he would simply try to love her without expectation that
she would reciprocate. When he needed a shoulder to lean on, he
would visit his brother or call his mom. It was terribly lonely at first.
He held her even when she was limp, caressed her even when she was
cold beneath his touch. He cried a lot, in private. But slowly, she
began to warm; in a year's time she had returned from the emotional
death that had threatened to engulf her. And in her heart she knew
she would not have made it back without him.

Other babies did come, another boy and a girl. The girl was a
charming, energetic, and happy child, but the boy was slow and shy,
and in his adolescence became sullen and rebellious. He crashed the
car a couple of times, was arrested for petty vandalism, gave little
thought to schoolwork. John was beside himself with frustration and
pain over it. He tried the strict disciplinarian's approach, but it only
made matters worse. Mary knew better. "You've got to talk to him,"
she would say. "He's got to know you love him." He had never been
comfortable with displays of emotion between men. He had never
even learned to hug his brother, the man he trusted most in the world.
But he knew she was right, and so he tried. He took his son out for ice
cream or to the ball game, and would try to talk. It was horribly awkward, filled with leaden silences. Late at night, in their bedroom he
would rant to Mary about sending the boy off to a military academy,
but she ignored the threat. "Keep trying," she would say gently. "He
needs to be loved." With her encouragement he persisted, even
attending counseling with the boy. Eventually it came out the young
man felt he could never replace the little boy who had died and that
he felt eclipsed by his bright-eyed sister in the affection of his parents,
especially Dad. Awkward silences remained, but after that confession,
there were no more car crashes, no more arrests. The boy's grades
climbed slowly. He even smiled once in a while. One day, after he had
been admitted to college, the boy hugged his dad and said simply,
"Thanks, Pa." "Thank your mother," John replied. "Without her, I
wouldn't have had a clue."

There were other crises in their lives: her new career after the children left home, which he found completely disorienting; his retirement, which drove her crazy until he finally figured out what to do with himself. And then, finally, her cancer. She fought bravely, but eventually it became clear she would lose the battle. She was suprisingly calm. He, on the other hand, was beside himself. One day she gave him a letter, which she told him not to open until she was gone. As she slipped it into his hand, he buried his head in her breast and wept uncontrollably. A week later she died, clutching his hand. As he sat waiting for the hospital chaplain, he opened the letter. "Beloved husband," she wrote, "Do you remember that wonderful novel by Robertson Davies, *The Lyre of Orpheus*? In it the main character, Simon Darcourt, makes a comment about marriage that I've never forgotten. Marriage, he says, isn't just domesticity, or the continuance of the race, or institutionalized sex, or a form of property right. And it damned well isn't happiness, as the word is generally used. I think it's a way of finding your soul. Well, my dearest, I have found my soul, and she is lodged forever in your heart. When I am gone, do not weep for me too long, for I will always be there with you, and you with me. I love you, just as you have loved me. Your Mary." It was a letter he would keep next to him for the rest of his life, in a little plastic case. Even when he went to bed he would take it with him in the breast pocket of his pajamas. When he himself died of a stroke four years later, the letter was buried with him, right next to her. Their son and daughter visited the grave a week later. They left a poem by Wendell Berry, taped to the tombstone. "They lived long, and were faithful," it read, "To the good in each other./They suffered as their faith required./Now their union is consummate/in earth, and the earth/is their communion. They enter/the serene gravity of the rain,/the hill's passage to the sea./After long striving, perfect ease."

John and Mary were born in my imagination, but they are composites of real flesh-and-blood people I have known who embody the love their story proclaims. In the Gospel lesson, Jesus declares that if we love him, we will obey his commandments and he will send a Spirit of truth to be with us. And the Epistle states explicitly that this love is a matter of action, not talk or theory. It is something that is done, something that is willed. But the relation between love and action, between love and obedience to God's commandments is subtle and complex. Love is not a matter of doing everything right. It is not a matter of "being good." Following God's rules in no way constitutes love. And yet, because it is an act of the will, it does involve doing more than feeling. John and Mary abide with one another in love in spite of feelings of anger, sorrow, and hurt. Nonetheless, it is not completely unrelated to feeling either. No one wants to be the "love project" of a person whose motive is to make him—or herself feel good about his or her capacity to love. What we do want is to be cared about. We want others to truly desire the good for us and to put that desire into action, even when it might cost dearly. We want their love to come from the heart.

It is from our parents that we first learn to love, first by experiencing their love for us, then by observing their love for each other. To the extent that the love fails, as it inevitably does, it is that much more difficult to learn to love. Marriage is therefore a primer, a textbook of love, from which we all take our lessons. The bonds of love in marriage, its intimacy and warmth, should not be seen as an insulation against a heartless world, but, as theologian Sebastian Moore puts it, as "a wholesome contagion in a heartless world." "This primordial intimacy," he writes, "has been since the beginning of time public and acclaimed and creates what we call a home, not only for children, but also for neighbors and, in some radiant instances—though not often, in our culture—for anyone in need of food and human comfort."

So I hold up to you the possibilities of this love rooted in marriage, in the hope you see in it possibilities for yourself and others. The love of a John and Mary, a love that is faithful to the good in each other, as the poet puts it, is a love obedient to the Great Commandment, a love that loves as Christ loved us, a sacrificial love. As Wendell Berry wrote to his wife, Tanya, "It is to be broken. It is to be torn open. It is not to be reached and come to rest in ever. I turn against you. I break from you. I turn to you. We hurt, and are hurt, and have each other for healing. It is a healing. It is never whole."

Healing. And when it heals, the scars that form are stronger than the bonds of the whole and sin-free love we knew in Eden. The wounds are made beautiful, like the stigmata of Christ, wounds that heal the world. It is resurrected love, love that has conquered even death.

Credentials

The Rev. William Hethcock

Galatians 1:18-2:10

∞

I

Paul is disappointed and disturbed, even "perplexed" (Galatians 4:20), by the news he hears from the churches in Galatia. Paul is "astonished." He sounds brokenhearted. He has himself been one or two times to preach and teach in Galatia. He is confident that he has been faithful in giving the Galatians the gospel he knows so well.

But now news has come to him saying that his friends in the Galatian churches have been listening to persons whom Paul sees as agitators and corruptors, preachers who have contaminated his gospel message with a notion of Christ's teaching that is contrary to the word Paul himself gave them there. Paul has been a champion of the mission to the Gentiles, but those who have preached in Galatia during his absence have been requiring the people to submit to circumcision, a strictly Jewish custom. Paul learns that these preachers have been saying in Galatia that no one may be a Christian without first submitting to Jewish traditions. The dreadful part of what this means is that the Galatians are returning to submission to the law. They have given up what they heard preached by Paul. They have forgotten that they are no longer under the law, but they are under grace, and their righteousness comes from trusting, believing with faith in Jesus Christ.

Paul is upset. Some might even perceive that Paul is angry.

II

And so Paul is writing a letter to the Galatians, and he is on the offensive. "Look, Galatians," he says, "this is Paul talking to you. Remember? I'm the one who came among you and preached the gospel of grace. You are no longer under the law but you are under grace. Remember?

And remember also, Galatians, I had checked out my preaching with the authorities in Jerusalem. Yes. Three years after I came to know Jesus as Lord on the road to Damascus, I went to Jerusalem to get to know the apostle Peter. For fifteen days we talked about the ways in which we know the Lord. And I went from Peter preaching and teaching, and I heard that even those who never saw me, but knew of my persecuting Christians in the past, were praising God because of my work in Jesus' name.

And then, Galatians, fourteen years after my conversion, Barnabas, Titus, and I went to Jerusalem where I laid out before the Christian authorities there the very gospel that I had preached to you. And again James and Peter and John, the acknowledged pillars there, recognized the grace that had been given to me to preach, and so they gave to Barnabas and me the right hand of fellowship. They were to continue preaching to the Jews and I to the Gentiles.

Paul wants the Galatians, whose new understanding of the teaching he himself is criticizing, to be aware that his words, the gospel as he preached it, were authentic, true, and worthy. Paul, though not one of the twelve himself, has his own apostolic credentials in place. His conversations are a part of those credentials. His conversation with Peter for fifteen days included consultation, teaching, and learning. And his later visit with the Jerusalem authorities gained him further authentication. Paul knows the gospel, and his credentials are up to date and in place.

III

Paul must have thought that this defense of his credentials would reinforce what he had preached to the Galatians. Credentials are important. Credentials have to do with your transcript, your resume, your life experience, and the things you can write and say about how you got wherever it is that you are. Sometimes people want to know your credentials before they trust you, and so Paul is telling about his credentials. Paul knows that credentials are important.

I wish you could see the academic and commencement ceremonies at Sewanee, where some of us attending this conference live. Perhaps they are similar at your school. Our faculty of 125 or so line up and process in all their regalia. They are beautiful and impressive, showing as they do their color-coded academic specialties and the levels of their highest degrees. This must be a great school, you might think, with such an array of academic credentials. People trust good credentials.

Have you ever noticed how almost everybody who has surgery boasts of having had the best doctor in the field? You hear them say, "Why, yes, I had the best specialist there is." "I had the very best cancer doctor around—specializes in treating just exactly what I was diagnosed as having." You never hear anyone say something like, "Well, my doctor's credentials weren't the best, but I went along with him anyway. One doctor is as good as another."

My wife and I can never find a really good heat pump specialist. The air conditioning never works right. We're always asking our friends, "Have you found good air conditioning people lately? We have had really lousy repair persons, and we are fed up. We want the best." We aren't looking for someone who knows how to fix only every other machine or who will tell us, "Well, it may work or it may not." We want someone with the best repair credentials we can find.

Parish search committees are always looking for the best priest to be their rector. They go over resumes and computer printouts for hours. They interview diligently and rigorously. No congregation wants a make-do, somewhat adequate, just average priest. They want the one with the best credentials for the position they describe.

Credentials are important. That's why everyone here in this room is engaged in gaining or improving our learning and preparation so that when the opportunity comes, we will be able to produce the right credentials for the task.

People tend to trust people with good credentials, someone well trained and equipped for the job at hand. Paul knows that, so he reassures those wayward Galatians that his credentials for his apostolic preaching of the gospel are tried and approved. I'm not just any preacher, Galatians. I'm the famous Paul, formerly Saul, converted and changed on the road to Damascus and approved and accredited by Peter and the other apostles right there in Jerusalem, the hub of the whole Christian movement. I am no jackleg missionary. I have a Ph.D., a red shirt, and a clerical collar. I'm the real thing. You can trust me on that, Galatians.

IV

But Paul was no fool, you know, because Paul had something else. And that something else was more important than his Jerusalem credentials. Paul could play the credentials game when it was necessary, but he had something more to say, and that was the heart of his apologia to the mulish and unmanageable Galatians. Paul knew the gospel of Jesus Christ, and that is what he had preached in their churches.

Paul had worked to rescue the people of Galatia from the secular and religious authority of the age and to bring them into the freedom they could know in the dominion of Christ. Paul is "astonished" that the Galatians who have heard him preach are "so quickly deserting the one who called [them] in the grace of Christ and are turning to a different gospel." They are following some new preachers "who [are] confusing [them] and who want to pervert the gospel of Christ." Paul had spoken strongly in his preaching, not because his message had been verified by some worldly authority or even by holy persons who were his companions in preaching Christ. Paul was not depending upon even these credentials. Paul had spoken strongly because he was called by Jesus Christ to preach a freedom from the law. Paul was charged to call humankind to a life of grace that would come to them if they would only believe the Christ and accept this free gift. Paul's credentials were not merely from his noteworthy contemporaries in the faith. Paul's credentials were from his Lord.

V

I wonder whether Paul succeeded in correcting the misguidance of his Galatian friends. We really don't know. It would do me a lot of good to know that he did indeed succeed in persuading them. But we don't know whether the Galatians listened to Paul, rejecting the preaching they had heard from others and returning to the gospel of grace that Paul had preached to them. Maybe they did, and maybe they didn't.

What we do know is that Paul was faithful. Paul was faithful to the authority given him by God. He was faithful to his calling to preach the gospel as it had been revealed to him. Paul's credentials, the most important credentials, the credentials he counted on to preach boldly and faithfully, were not those he received from those around him in the church.

And so the message for us hidden in Paul's letter to the Galatians is not a message about how the people responded to Paul. It is not a message about gathering together a resume of impressive wordly credentials. The message for us in the letter Paul wrote is the example Paul gives through himself.

This is the truth that comes to us. After all our necessary approvals are in place, after all our academic certificates have been endorsed and presented to us, after they have been framed and are displayed on the wall, after we find ourselves placed in a position in which our ministry is recognized and our role is spelled out for us, after all our dreams of who and what we want to be seem to be coming true, what is required of us is not our faithfulness to these wordly human credentials, but our faithfulness to the gospel we have received. Paul says to us, "I want you to know, brothers and sisters, that the gospel that was proclaimed by me is not of human origin; for I did not receive it from a human source, nor was I taught it, but I received it through a revelation of Jesus Christ."

What we know for certain is that Paul, with all that had been given him to encourage him in his preaching, even association with other apostles who approved his message, what really gave him the strength to persevere was his certainty in the revelation he had received from Jesus Christ. The same has been true for every preacher through the ages. The authority to preach that has come to them all is that same gospel revelation. And what we may know with certainty is that the same revelation is power and strength enough for you and me.

Defenders of Ambiguity

The Rev. J. Donald Waring, Rector
St. Thomas Episcopal Church, Terrace Park, Ohio

∞

Thus Abraham "believed God, and it was reckoned to him as righteous-ness." So then, those who are people of faith are blessed with Abraham who had faith. (Galatians 3:6, 9)

I have lately encountered a character called the Grand Inquisitor, who makes his appearance in a novel, *The Brothers Karamazov*, by Dostoyevsky. The Grand Inquisitor is an aged, Roman Catholic cardinal, living in Spain during the time of the Inquisitions. It is he who presides over the rooting out, the arresting, the interrogating, and the burning of heretics.

It so happens that Christ himself makes a visit to this particular place at this particular time. He comes not in glorious majesty, but *"softly, unobserved, and yet, strange to say, everyone recognizes him."* People flock to him. He gives sight to a blind man, and life to a dead child. The Grand Inquisitor watches Christ, then arrests him and locks him in a dungeon. On the night before he is to have this visitor burned at the stake, the Grand Inquisitor comes to the cell to give Jesus a piece of his mind. He is furiously angry at Christ for leaving the world in such an ill-defined mess, for leaving people with decisions to make that they are not capable of making, for leaving people with room for doubt instead of certainty, hunger instead of bread, confusion instead of happiness, questions instead of answers. The Grand Inquisitor will burn Christ at the stake, and then get on with the business of keeping order. He says finally to Jesus:

> *We shall allow or forbid them to live with their wives and mistresses, to have or not to have children—according to whether they have been obedi-ent or disobedient—and they will submit to us gladly and cheerfully. The most painful secrets of their conscience, all, all they bring to us, and we shall have an answer for all. And they will be glad to believe our answer, for it will save them from the great anxiety and terrible agony they endure at present in making a free decision for themselves. And all will be happy, all the millions of creatures except the hundred thousand who rule over them. For only we, we who guard the mystery, shall be unhappy.*

Although most of us would certainly side with Christ in this drama, still the Grand Inquisitor makes an understandable point. Christ has left this world in a mess. We live in a time of subtle yet tremendous confusion. In the onrush of the secular world, centuries-old understandings of belief in God and personal conduct are crumbling before us. We would like Jesus to come and clear things up, straighten things out, and give us the answers to the vexing questions before us. Come, Jesus, and tell us definitively about the sanctity of life. Come, Jesus, and clear up the mystery of human sexuality. Come, Jesus, and explain to us the mystery of suffering. Better yet, come and do away with suffering; nobody likes it, anyway. Come, Jesus, and give us clear direction and guidance for our personal lives. I mean, what is to be gained by allowing us to make bad decisions, work in the wrong careers, marry the wrong spouses, and buy stock in the wrong companies? Do you remember the lament of the Psalmist? *"What profit is there in my death, if I go down to the Pit? Will the dust praise thee? Will it tell of thy faithfulness? Hear, O Lord, and be gracious to me! O Lord, be thou my helper!" (Psalm 30:9-10)* Come, Jesus, tell us what to do.

This was how it worked back in the days of the Bible, was it not? When you needed direction and guidance you got a burning bush, a parted sea, a star in the sky, or the decisive proclamation of a prophet. I remember as a child thinking how lucky those people were to have God just popping by from time to time to tell them exactly what to do. Consider tonight's appointed reading from the Book of Deuteronomy (16:18-20; 17:14-20). We have heard in the Mosaic Law God's instruction that the people should appoint judges and officers in all the towns. And over all the cities and towns they are to set a king that the Lord will choose. Granted, this king and the officers are to judge the people with righteous judgment: justice and only justice shall they follow. But they will be making the decisions. They will be making things very clear for the people and spelling out the will of God for them in every detail. Of course, this leaves little room for Anglican ambiguity, but that's all right: the people will not have to endure the great anxiety and terrible agony of making too many free decisions for themselves.

Throughout all the twists and turns of life we look to God and to our faith communities for guidance. In some traditions God's guidance will be funneled to the people through mediums that are declared infallible or inerrant: a pope, the Bible, a modern-day prophet. The Episcopal Church, on the other hand, has the peculiar talent for giving you a "definite maybe" on whatever you might ask.

The Episcopal Church often infuriates people—both our own and those not our own—who want clear answers. It has been said of us that we spend so much time questioning answers that we never get around to answering questions. Our Anglican ambiguity is both a blessing and a curse; it is a blessing because it allows people the space to work things through for themselves and become personally invested in their faith; it allows for mystery. It is a also a curse, however, because the Grand Inquisitors of the world have us surrounded, and they seem to be speaking the loudest. They are the heavy handed fundamentalists to the right of us; they are the equally intolerant politically correct thought police to the left of us. Their judgments on issues are often far less than life giving; they are at times death dealing. And all too often the people in between are happy to believe whatever they are told.

Now bring all this to bear on our calling as priests and preachers in the Anglican tradition. One way to go is to be like the Grand Inquisitor: Guard the mystery, clear it up, spell it out, smooth it over, have an answer for everything, and relieve people of that great anxiety and terrible agony that comes from wrestling faithfully toward and faithfully within their own relationship with Christ. And make no mistake about it: many would like to be relieved of that burden and have someone else carry it for them. People these days are not breaking down church doors in search of ambiguity and mystery. They want moral and theological certainty. The trouble with that is: If you have certainty, you don' t need faith.

Our calling is different. Our calling is not to be guardians of mystery but rather, defenders of the space that allows people to confront mystery—the mystery of God and life and death. People need space to work out their faith in fear and trembling. People need space to confront the outrage of their mortality and grapple with its mysteries and awful empty possibilities without being told too quickly to look on the bright side of life. Nobody can tell you what to think, or how to feel, or what to do when you are staring into these unknowns. So it is precisely the space of ambiguity and uncertainty that we are to defend. That is where faith in God becomes possible—in the ambiguous, in the uncertain.

Consider Abraham, who stared into the mystery of faith. Consider the great anxiety and terrible agony of his faith journey to Mount Moriah. No Grand Inquisitor would have let him go on it, that's for sure. Abraham would have been spared that journey. Was he full of certainty on the way? Were he and Isaac singing rousing choruses of "Blessed Assurance" on the way? I don't think so. As far as Abraham knew, he was about to lose everything that was precious to him. Yet, he was willing to take that journey. Paul says that Abraham had only one thing on the way: faith. Abraham's journey required his fearful and unsteady interpretations of faith. And that's why God declared him righteous: because he believed, though he did not see (Galatians 3:6).

I think what God asked of Abraham is the same thing God asked of the judges and kings of Israel. And it is the same thing God asks of us: to live by faith, not with certainty. Oh, what an unpopular message to preach. Why preach it? Why faith instead of certainty? Because God has no wish to frighten us into recognition of him, and no desire to impress us into worshiping him. Instead, he comes to us *softly and unobserved*. Instead, he has left our minds totally free to choose. That is the only way we can freely return God's love, which I believe is God's purpose for our creation. This way of grace is God's absolute risk that we will all not take him seriously and deem other pursuits to be more worthy of our time and attention. But it is a risk God is apparently willing to take.

Here is a story* I recently read that may be helpful for some. For the Grand Inquisitors of the world and those who wish to follow them, I am afraid this will be entirely unhelpful.

It seems that a priest of the church by the name of Homer faced a major decision in his life. He prayed incessantly for a sign, a signal, a star in the sky, a word from the pulpit, something, anything that would give him direction: "Show me the way; tell me what to do; give me the answer!" No answer from God was forthcoming, and Homer's anxiety and agony knew no bounds.

Undaunted, Homer continued with his prayers; he stormed the throne of heaven day and night pleading for an answer. Finally, after many weeks of this, God spoke to him loud and clear, and this is what Homer reports having heard:

"Homer, I don't really care on this one! Make your decision faithfully, and I will be with you!"

Shocking, isn't it, that God would treat us like adults and expect us to behave in like manner? It just may be that Christ has left us with that much freedom.

The question is, Do you want it?

*The story is told by the Very Rev. Alan Jones in a sermon titled "Born Again!," printed in *Pulpit Digest*, March/April 1994.

And the Watching-Women Say Amen

Joy E. Rogers

Matthew 13: 31-33

∞

For centuries, in the remote highlands of Scotland, people in isolated villages have waited upon the infrequent and irregular visits of clergy to perform the sacramental chores that tie up the loose ends of human existence in an ecclesiastically approved manner. When a child is born, if the child survives, there will be a church baptism when the priest next visits. But life and death and God wait for no man. When a woman is giving birth, a community gathers.

From the diary of a Scottish Midwife:

When the image of the God of life is born into the world I put three little drops of water on the child's forehead. I put the first little drop in the name of the Father, and the watching-women say Amen. I put the second little drop in the name of the Son, and the watching-women say Amen. I put the third little drop in the name of the Spirit, and the watching women say Amen. And I beseech the Holy Three to lave and to bathe the child and to preserve it to Themselves. And the watching-women say Amen. All the people in the house are raising their voices with the watching-women, giving witness that the child has been committed to the blessed Trinity. By the Book itself! Ear has never heard music more beautiful than the music of the watching women when they are consecrating the seed of man and committing him to the great God of life (The Celtic Vision: Selections from the Carmina Gadelica, edited by Esther de Waal. St. Bede's Publications, Petersham, Massachusetts, 1988, 111).

The kingdom of God is like. . .

All the world's great religious traditions (Buddhism, Islam, Judaism, Hinduism, no less than Christianity) have a public face, the official realm of entrenched hierarchies, where doctrines are debated and promulgated, the great rituals lavishly performed, where great heroes are enshrined in stained glass and stone, and portraits of lesser heroes decorate the walls and dining halls of institutional life.

But in every corner of the globe, within the homes of human beings and by the hearth, the great tradition is supplemented and subverted by what is sometimes called the little tradition. Here is a realm of household gods and homage due to ancestors; the rites that accompany the ordinary round—the birthing of babes, and the deaths of ordinary folk—folk who are neither prelates nor monarchs; chants and prayers crooned to attend the catching of fish, the preparing of food, the weaving of cloth, the building of homes.

A pervasive, inclusive, surprising—even unseemly, inconsistent, somewhat superstitious—way to God, some may say. Yet faith that finds God in the baking of bread, and the sowing of seed, the kingdom of heaven is like.

Faith enough to find God present to all of life; compassion that seeks God's face in others; the hope that knows that God is working in tedious chores and daily routines, in the commonplace tragedies or the ordinary miracles of all human existence. Even courage to defy institutions when they prefer the abstraction of issues to the complexity of persons.

A great tradition legitimates a preacher—the authority shown in collars and chasubles and chalices; authority credentialed by theological degrees, tested by ecclesastical protocols, and conferred by a bishop's special touch; authority to preside at an altar, to preach from a pulpit, high and lifted up. A great tradition gives a preacher form and limits for our speaking, gives shape to our thinking and edges to our believing.

A great tradition has grown out of the preaching and teaching of a little man from a backwater town in the Galilee. A small-town carpenter named Jesus from Nazareth sowed a rich harvest of Jesus stories; some he told, some they told about him—little traditions that gave rise to those four extravagant Gospels that shelter and sustain a church, in which birds like us may find a home.

In them, Jesus points us still to God; not God set apart and far away, not a God only to be worshiped and adored, debated and defined. But God, known and named, God, tasted and touched, in the company of others, in the midst of the mess, in all the mystery of creaturely existence, most of all in the messy mystery of death.

For leaven, is after all, only dead bread—the moldering, decaying bit of old dough, stashed in a dark and hidden place. And from such a dying comes energy and power to raise the rest of the sodden lump. It is a little tradition recipe for salvation, from Jesus himself, and it carries the seed of a great tradition.

Into the stuff of the world, a Bakerwoman God hides a bit of dead bread. Just add water, the waters of creation, of baptism, of birthing, even the tears of your grief and sorrow.

Work it through with the muscle that only flesh and blood can provide, so that no bit of existence is now untouched by this churning, fermenting newness, and it is inextricably one with all of it.

Now you can't tell that it is even there, and so you wait. The process takes time; it can be as boring as watching paint dry, or grass grow, as tedious as loving, or dying, when there is no evidence that anything good will come of the prospect.

The actions involved are ordinary, common, domestic, yet expansive, and so is the intended product. Our baker is making no holy food for Passover seders, not with all that leaven. Nor is this a gourmet pastry for an exclusive dinner party. She is making a substantial quantity of quite ordinary bread—filling, nourishing, and it will feed lots and lots of hungry, ordinary people.

The presence of warm air does seem to speed up the process of fermentation, breaking down sticky barriers, creating new spaces within the loaf, and lightening the product.

The end result of a silent presence, an invisible energy, and a passionate effort is an unmistakeable rising in our midst.

Such, says the man with the parables, is like the kingdom of God. And he must know, for he is the source of the ongoing, churning fermentation that reveals the presence of the kingdom among us; he is the leaven for our kingdom bread and the yeast that transforms the fruit of the vine into the blood red wine of our salvation.

And he asks the likes of us to join him on his dying rising way.

My sisters and brothers, you too are bakers and bearers and birthers, a company of sowers and midwives, who receive with great care and much hope the truths of a great tradition.

Bring all of who you are, and who you are called to become, to the task. Out of your experience, relationships, imaginations, give little traditions voice and visibility in the public arena; point to the workings of God in people's lives and in this tired old world; and bring to speech the hunger for God in human hearts. Like he did; because he did.

Raise up for us all a vision of an ordinary realm emerging in our midst, a realm where justice and compassion, wholeness, healing, forgiveness, and peace are the stuff of ordinary existence and the lot of ordinary people.

By your words and wisdom, by your prayer and care, consecrate all of creation, "by the Book itself," and commit yourselves, your passions, and your preaching, to the great God of life.

"And the watching-women say Amen."

Preaching at the Eucharist

William Hethcock, Professor of Homiletics
The School of Theology of the University of the South
Sewanee, Tennessee

[This talk is based on an article that appeared in the Sewanee
Theological Review, 39 (Easter 1996) 2.]

∞

I think all of us know that there has been a revolution in preaching in
our country since about 1972, when Professor Fred Craddock published his first edition of *As One Without Authority*. That seems to me to
be the pivotal book, the one that started the torrent of great writing
about preaching over the past twenty-five years. I suspect that you
read a good many of these authors in your courses and that you join
me in being under the influence of outstanding homiletical personalities such as Eugene Lowry, David Buttrick, Charles Rice, Thomas
Long, and Fred Craddock himself. Where would we be if it were not
for all those greats?

But among that list of homileticists whom we read, only one, Rice,
is actually a member of what we might call the liturgical church. What
I am pointing out is that regardless of how much we appreciate and
admire their writings, the main resources we use for our work in our
Episcopal seminaries are devised by people who are quite likely to see
their sermons as events that are related to a very free form of Sunday
morning worship. The sermon about which these authors are writing
is a longer event, often comprising most of the worship time and
often functioning as the central happening of the hour.

We Episcopalians tend to think of preaching at a more liturgical
form of the Holy Eucharist as it is celebrated by Roman Catholics,
Lutherans, and Anglicans. Our sermons are set in the context of a pre-
scribed liturgy. While preachers in other Christian communities might
feel cramped or limited by our liturgical boundaries, we Episcopalians
tend to like it the way we have it with a Prayer Book that guides us in
our planning of worship and our crafting of sermons. We have something different in mind about preaching from that which is in the
minds of those helpful authors when they craft sermons to be given
from their own pulpits. While we are thriving on the priceless studies
and writings of our Christian neighbors, we find ourselves having to
adapt here and there what we are hearing from them so that we may

make good use of their method in our own liturgical setting.

A student brought to me for my comment a tape of a sermon she had preached in a field education parish. The sermon began, "In a few moments, our service will continue, but first, I want to speak in this sermon about . . . " Suddenly I was aware once again of an old problem that has plagued Episcopalians for decades. We preachers sometimes fail to see the unity between the sermon we have crafted and the Eucharistic liturgy that will surround it. Unless we are careful, we will suspend our attention to the liturgy we are celebrating and deal with the sermon as an interruption, something that interferes with the liturgical setting. A preacher who is thinking this way is quite likely to give the congregation a sermon that is indeed an interruption and interference. What I am suggesting in this lecture is that we need to be aware of the close relationship between word and sacrament intended by our Prayer Book. We need to be aware of the setting in which we are preaching. With these concerns in mind, we need to craft our sermons with care that will help them to rest comfortably in their liturgical setting and to become "of a piece" with the Eucharistic liturgy.

After thinking about this point through several years of teaching, I decided to look around to see whether anyone else is concerned about the same thing. I discovered that Roman Catholic homileticists looked at this issue at Vatican II and carefully addressed the subject of the homily and its relationship to the Mass. W. J. O'Shea comments, "It is important to see the relationship between the homily and the celebration of the mystery . . . They are in fact two aspects of the one celebration, . . . part of the liturgy itself, . . . part of the liturgical service."[1] Gerald S. Sloyan, also a Roman Catholic, describes liturgical preaching similarly. He writes, "In brief, liturgy is a living presentation of the received word of God as worship, its translation into deed. Liturgical preaching is the biblical preaching that fits into that matrix."[2]

Before we talk specifically about how to preach in the context of the Eucharist, let's take a look at our liturgy. One of the exciting things about our Prayer Book is that the services in it are very well organized. What is your definition of worship? A "working definition" I am using as I speak to you is this: Worship is a human activity with a purpose and direction bringing us into the unique experience of the presence of God. A good scriptural definition may be the offertory sentence from Psalm 96:8: "Ascribe to the Lord the honor due his Name; bring offerings and come into his courts." Of course, the central and important offering we bring at the Eucharist is ourselves.

I maintain that in our Prayer Book all acts of liturgical worship to be so called have one central characteristic in common. I have come to call it by my own term, the "liturgical principle." The principle dictates that worship always begins with a congregation of people who are in one given state or circumstance. Of course, each person's situation is unique, but all together make one given condition. Worship is entered into from the unity created by this often scattered perspective.

Liturgical worship calls on worshipers to surrender their situations and to enter into a moving and living process, part intellectual and part emotional, during which change can come about. At the end of the worship time, worshipers leave the worship place in a new state, a new condition, which is different from the condition with which they entered the experience. The liturgical principle is that worship is an event designed to change the situation of those who enter into it.

Gwen Kennedy Neville and John H. Westerhoff III have formalized this kind of worship happening in a description of what they call a "transition rite," which they recognize as an anthropological process. Persons enter into the rite in a given "old status" or "role." They "separate" from this role in preparation for a "transition." A "reincorporation" occurs, and they enter into a new "status" or "role."[3]

The simplest and most obvious examples of this characteristic of worship happen at a marriage or a baptism. At a marriage, a man and a woman enter the church as single persons. The liturgy tells everyone what is about to happen and what it means. The couple declare their intentions, exchange vows, and, after a blessing and perhaps the Eucharist, they leave the church in a different relationship to each other, their families, and everyone else. At a baptism, adults come or an infant is brought to the font, where after vows are taken, the candidate receives the gift of baptism. The newly baptized leaves the church in a new state, a new relationship with God and the world.

This liturgical principle is at work at the Eucharist as well. We enter into the service needing renewal, refreshment, and challenge. We hear Scripture and a sermon, we respond with the Creed and the prayers, we participate in the Great Thanksgiving, we make our communion, and we depart with a renewed readiness "to do the work (God has) given us to do." The sermon preached within the context of that happening is not only in touch with the theme suggested by the readings and the season, but it is crafted in a way that contributes to the logical flow of the liturgy and participates in the celebration the congregation is making together. On the one hand, this may sound like a limiting view of the homiletical possibilities at the Eucharist. Actually, however, this concern for the setting in which the sermon is preached may open vast possibilities for the meaning and power of worship that are limited when the sermon's context is ignored.

Having said these things, I am going to suggest to you ten guidelines that may be helpful to you in preparing sermons to be preached at the Eucharist. These ideas have been tested through ten years of student preaching in classroom and chapel at our seminary. Not all students agree with all of them. There is probably something here to offend everyone. But I propose that these guidelines do offer a starting place for those who want sermon and liturgy to be woven together in a reverent and helpful way. These suggestions are made with the hope that you will adapt them to your own preaching style. Although they are worded dogmatically, they are intended to be used with the preacher's discretion and good judgment. They are guidelines, not laws.

1. Look at the liturgy as a whole. The season and the reading on which you plan to preach will suggest a theme to be carried out in the selection of the liturgical options, the music, and all other components. How can the sermon participate in that theme with language, tone, ideas, and proclamation? It is never good to surrender the sermon time to some other pursuit than preaching the gospel message. Notice the flow of the liturgy, and allow the sermon to become a part of it. Especially, allow nothing to take place between the Gospel and the beginning of the sermon, certainly not a hymn.

2. Give careful attention to appropriate beginnings. The moment the gospel ends and the people sit down is the moment when they are most likely to be ready to listen. Crank-up palaver designed to win your listeners' affection or to convince them you are a regular person is especially out of touch with the liturgical setting. Informality is often appropriate; irrelevant chatter is not. Introductions are unnecessary. Your opening word is best designed to gain attention to something important in respect to the focus of the sermon itself. Either exegesis of the Scripture or a recalling of the human condition will make the best beginning.

3. Avoid opening acclamations and opening prayers. Traditions of long standing lead us to assume that no sermon may be safely begun

without some personal prayer or an invocation of the Trinity. The people already know we are religious, and many of them are trying hard not to hold that against us. Why remind them unnecessarily? Leonel L. Mitchell observes, "Often sermons begin with a prayer or the invocation 'In the Name of the Father, and of the Son, and of the Holy Spirit,' although some preachers feel that this usage separates the sermon from the rest of the liturgy and prefer to begin directly."[4] We have discovered in our chapel that a direct move from the gospel to the first sentence of the sermon is better uninterrupted by a moment of pious prayer from the preacher. The preacher motions to the people to sit and begins the sermon with a carefully planned opening sentence. That's all that is needed.

4. Avoid the intrusion of the self. For some reason, clergy like to tell from the pulpit incidents from their own personal stories (as well as their family's!), and for some reason, their congregations tire of listening to them. All clergy will speak of their feelings and their responses to situations around us all, but bringing illustrative stories about one's personal life or family experiences is a distraction from the people's experience of the Gospel. Sermons authenticated by the advice or career of the preacher are usually heard as parent-to-child communications, and the evaluation of students listening to each other preach has indicated to me that such sermons do not accomplish their goals. Listeners prefer to be led to new decision making on their own in lieu of hearing even the best intended clerical advice. A sermon is authenticated twice, once by the Scripture on which it is based and again by the experience of the listeners. The preacher is a conduit, not a guru. The priest's personal witness to the truth of the gospel is important. The priest's personal intrusion of self into the liturgy is out of place.

5. Proclaim the gospel inherent in the chosen reading. Our sermons preached in the context of the Eucharist should be based on one or two of the readings for the day. The gospel proclaimed in those readings authenticates, as noted earlier, what we are going to say. From time to time, thematic or topical sermons of interest or concern to the congregation may be appropriate, but, generally, the sermon should proclaim the gospel truth in the readings. Reginald Fuller has said, "The purpose of the sermon is to extract from the scripture readings the essential core and content of the gospel, to penetrate behind the day's pericope to the proclamation of the central act of God in Christ which it contains, in

order that the central act of God can be made the material for recital in the prayer of thanksgiving."[5]

6. Recall with the congregation the human condition. The gospel inherent in the reading either contains a human condition, addresses a human condition, or both. That is to say that Jesus or Paul, for example, know a situation that exists among those to whom they are speaking in a given reading, and they are speaking to that human condition. For example, on his journey to Jerusalem, Jesus is speaking to his disciples who do not understand him. He is addressing their human condition. At the same time, Mark is reporting Jesus' words for another audience who will hear the gospel read to them, and Mark is addressing their human condition. What is the human condition in the congregation to which the sermon is addressed, and how can Jesus' words be proclaimed to them where they are here and now? Identification of the human condition is a part of every sermon. Discovering among ourselves our life situations analogous to those which the Bible addresses helps us to discern how the Bible speaks to us. Unless our situation is admitted intellectually, felt experientially, and owned honestly during the sermon, the proclamation the sermon makes may be information gratefully received, but it will not touch us with the good news as we long for it or as God intends it.

7. Use stories and illustrations with care. It is difficult to tell which is more harmful to the sermon's cogency, including an illustration with too few of the details or one with so much information that the effort to make the sermon's message clear is actually damaged. Moving in and out of a story is a delicate moment in crafting a sermon, and learning to do it well is an art. An illustrative story must fit what it is illustrating in every detail. It must have precisely the right strength, neither too strong or too weak. The subject matter of the illustration is sensitive to the worship setting and the flow of the Eucharistic liturgy. Humor is helpful for congregations that have learned to laugh, but knee-slapper stories become ends in themselves and disrupt listening and worship as well. One story or illustration well woven into the language of the sermon and referred to again as the sermon proceeds is frequently more effective for worshipful listening than several stories and wordy illustrations.

8. Become aware of the power of language. Prayer Book language is very beautiful in its simplicity, and so the best language for the pulpit is the same kind of simple language, well chosen and easily under-

stood. Preachers sometimes fear that simple language will require them to preach only simple sermons, but they delight in discovering that profound insights and provoking images may be accomplished with language that is readily understood at a high school student level, the level at which oral communication can most readily be heard and understood. A part of preparing to preach is planning the language and word choice that will most effectively get the message heard, as opposed to entering the pulpit with only an outline and "winging it." Congregations who are convinced that they prefer manuscript-free preachers, in my opinion, unwittingly deprive themselves of more effective preaching and worship when they deter their priest from learning to preach effectively with either good notes or a complete manuscript. The best preaching at the Eucharist is brought about by careful planning and intentional language. Only the most skilled preachers are able to speak well with no notes at all. Those who can should; those who can't will do well to develop manuscript preaching as a skill.

9. Know when to quit. Many congregations have time limits dictated by scheduled educational events. Aside from this restraint, a preacher should be sensitive to when what is intended to be said has been said. Every beginning preacher eventually asks, "How long should a sermon be?" The answer is that the sermon is as long as it feels. This sounds like avoiding the question, but that is not the intent. A carefully planned sermon with a goal clearly in the preacher's mind when it was crafted in the study will move smoothly, carefully, and directly toward its proclamation so well that listeners will be unaware of its length. The sermon will end when that point has been made. Anything further damages the power of the sermon and makes the congregation become restless or even annoyed.

We have all heard sermons we thought would never end. The problem frequently is not their length, but their design. One way to put it is to say that long homilies are homilies that seem long; short homilies are homilies that seem short. A sermon that goes on too long, one that keeps explaining its point, is like having a wonderful dinner in a restaurant ruined by a waiter who won't bring your check.

10. End the sermon with anticipation of what will follow. Just as the opening sentence of the sermon is carefully designed to gain attention and get moving, the closing sentence should be well designed to challenge the congregation with a gospel proclamation.

They should be able to discern clearly what they are either to know, what they are to do, or both. I have learned from students that the word "Amen" at the end of a sermon terminates all thought and consideration of what has been said. I have been brought to believe that the preacher is wise to allow the last sentence to rest in the minds of the listeners for a time of silence rather than giving an Amen or a prayer. The best-planned closing sentence will lead well to the next thing to be said: "We believe in one God."

The congregations to whom we preach need never know that we are attempting to craft our homilies with special attention to the worship setting. Planning carefully to preach at the Eucharist, however, has the potential of helping worship to become even more the sense-making and powerful dimension of human life today's worshipers need and deserve.

Notes

1. "Homily," New Catholic Encyclopedia, vol. 7 (Washington, D.C.: The Catholic University of America, 1967), 114.

2. Gerald S. Sloyan, "What Is Liturgical Preaching?" Liturgy 8, 2 (????): 11.

3. Gwen Kennedy Neville and John H. Westerhoff III, Learning Through Liturgy (New York: Seabury Press, 1978, 170-173).

4. Praying Shapes Believing: A Theological Commentary on the Book of Common Prayer (Harrisburg, PA: Morehouse Publishing, 1990), 136.

5. "What is Liturgical Preaching?" (London, SCM Press, Ltd., 1957), 22.

Some Closing Reflections

"With Groanings That Cannot Be Uttered"
Preaching as Communal Participation in Spirit-Prayer

∞

This is a book of preaching and about preaching. While it has made frequent reference to the witness of God's Spirit, it has nevertheless (inevitably) been deeply immersed in human language—sermon language and meta-sermon language (language *about* the language of sermons). The question at this point may well be, but *where*, exactly, is "the Word of the Lord," the witness of the Spirit, in the midst of all these many human words? Has all this multilayered sermon speech become, in fact, an end in itself, rather than a means to an end?

It is high time, therefore, to reaffirm explicitly the conviction that undergirds this book: The fundamental task of a preacher is not to fill space with *sacred words*, but rather to use words to *shape a sacred space*. Perhaps a lowly illustration will help to illuminate the difference between these two.

Joke telling is an art form (a truth to which those of us who do not tell jokes well can readily attest). A good joke teller uses words with care—and gesture, facial expression, body language, timing, and many other intuitive skills as well. All of these contribute to making a joke "work." And yet the laughter-igniting "spark" takes place *not* in the words or the gestures per se, nor in all of the skills combined. A joke is fostered by the teller's art, but it actually "happens" in the space between its teller and its hearers. If the hearers don't "get it," they *just don't get it*. (Have you ever tried to *explain* a joke to someone who missed its point in your telling, or sat through someone else's labored explanation of a joke you didn't get?)

The dance of the Spirit through the shape of a sermon may be something like that. If more theological language seems necessary here, perhaps we could put it this way: Preachers are charged with the responsibility of shaping an altar with their sermon work, but they can only hope and pray for the descent of Divine Fire upon that sermon altar. They never ignite the Fire. God's Word sacramentally inhabits human words, but no combination of human words can ever be equated with, or productive of, "The Word of the Lord."

This fact is one that preachers encounter time and again. It is a source both of frustration and of grace. The most careful sermon efforts sometimes (for whatever reason) seem to fall flat. Those who listened "just didn't get it." On the other hand, sermons after which a preacher may feel like crawling in a hole and hiding, sometimes touch hearts and transform lives, all at once, gradually over time, or in apparent spontaneous combustion at times and places far down the track from the original sermon setting.

Preaching, therefore, is not a vocation tailor-made for those whose sense of personal affirmation is built on predictable indicators of success. And yet there is this promise to those who try as best they can to preach in faith: God's Word will not return void; scattered seed will, in the fullness of time, find good soil and produce abundant fruit. The words of preaching, therefore, are *offered* words, not *magic* words. Offered words, however, become *efficacious* words through the witness of the Spirit, whose wind blows in, around, under, and about them.

That is all well and good, perhaps. But it doesn't seem to give the preacher much to go on when faced, over and again, with the fact that "Sunday is coming!" It is comforting to trust in the witness of the Spirit, and challenging to tune one's efforts to one's most attentive awareness to the Spirit's energy. But what is a preacher supposed to think when "they just don't get it"? What is a preacher supposed to do to help them try?

In some ways, this book as a whole tries to address that question, at least in part. What, exactly, does it try, by way of illustration, to suggest?

Listen to the conversations and to the conversation partners. Keep listening, preacher, even when *you* don't seem to "get it." Listen intently, but listen gently. Listen not so much for the "point" as for the *flow*. Do not search for snappy "sound bytes." Rather, position yourself to listen for subtle nuance and deep resonance. Don't listen for what sounds clever, or for what seems geared to produce neat, quick closure on ambiguity and complexity. Listen instead for what is surprising, unsettling, threatening, open-ended, mysterious. The words one hears in such places are less likely to be idolatrous, more likely to be the stuff of which icons are made.

Learning to pray is more a matter of listening than of speaking. Praying has more to do with sensing the eloquence in the quiet consensus of an earnest, reverent community than it does with producing the well-turned phrases of a single, vocal "expert." The only one who can effectively offer prayers *for* a community is one who is praying *in* and *with* a community.

St. Paul thus describes the elusive articulation of the Spirit in those joyful, perplexing, or tragic human situations that defy both description and explanation:

> *The Spirit helps us in our weakness; for we do not know how to pray as we ought, but that very Spirit intercedes with sighs too deep for words. And God, who searches the heart, knows what is the mind of the Spirit, because the Spirit intercedes for the saints according to the will of God.*

> *We know that all things work together for good for those who love God, who are called according to his purpose (Romans 8:26-28).*

Not much help, frankly, if one is looking for a by-the-numbers field manual, either for forming prayers or for assembling sermons. And yet Paul's words (God's words) shape a context for understanding what can happen when the processes of praying/preaching are faithfully undertaken.

Preaching is not about getting off, standing apart, figuring out something to say, about or on behalf of God, to passive listeners who need to be told a thing or two for their own spiritual good. Preaching is participating in the back-and-forth, the ebb and flow, the sprightly dance and stumbling shuffle of communion that is always going on between conversation partners.

Prayer, proclamation, and preaching—they are all ways of embodying the revelatory interchange that holds the world in being through the primordial power of the Spirit. The task of the praying preacher in community is simply this: to sense, share, and celebrate that power in an ongoing adventure of sacred conversation.